CHINA CRY

THE NORA LAM STORY

Nora Lam
with
Richard H. Schneider

THOMAS NELSON PUBLISHERS
NASHVILLE

Nora Lam International Ministries
P.O. Box 24466
San Jose, CA. 95154
(408) 629-5000

Copyright © 1991 by Trinity Christian Center of Santa Ana, Inc., and Nora Lam
Chinese Ministries International

Any name and/or other differences between *China Cry,* the book, and "China Cry,"
the film, are due to adaptations for the screen.

Published in Nashville, Tennessee, by Thomas Nelson, Inc., and distributed in Can-
ada by Lawson Falle, Ltd., Cambridge, Ontario.

Scripture quotations are from the NEW KING JAMES VERSION of the Bible.
Copyright © 1979, 1980, 1982, Thomas Nelson, Inc., Publishers.

Library of Congress Cataloging-in-Publication Data

Schneider, Dick, 1922–
    China cry : the Nora Lam story / Richard H. Schneider.
        p.   cm.
    Rev. ed. of: China cry / Nora Lam with Irene Burk Harrell. c1980.
    ISBN 0-8407-3187-6 (pb)
    1. Lam, Nora.   2. Evangelists—United States—Biography.
3. Christian biography—China.   I. Lam, Nora. China cry.
II. Title.
BV3785.L26S25   1991
269′.2′092—dc20
[B]   90-48450
                                                                         CIP

Printed in the United States of America

1 2 3 4 5 6 7 – 96 95 94 93 92 91

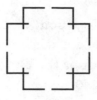

CONTENTS

PREFACE

Fasten your seatbelt and get ready to experience one of the most extraordinary dramas of our time! The true story of Nora Lam is more than just a "great read" or a wonderful motion picture. You'll find that it contains the power to transform your life too—just as it already has done for millions of others.

In a time when spiritual heroes are harder and harder to find, Nora Lam's amazing journey of faith continues to touch countless hearts. It speaks to anyone in need of fresh hope. Her story proves again that even in this age of human disbelief, the living God still intervenes in our everyday affairs.

Nora's account of God's power in the face of "impossible" odds is so powerful that we had to share it with the world. Thousands of TBN partners sacrificed to bring it to the screen. The result is now Hollywood history. The TBN film, *China Cry*, is already considered an inspirational classic by many film critics. Nora's story of faith is destined to reach billions around the globe with a message of victory and hope.

No circumstances—even political oppression, revolution, and war—can prevent the love and power of God from working in lives today. When you face your own personal hour of darkness and despair, all you need to do is call upon Him.

The *China Cry* story is true evidence that God is concerned about even the most minute details in our lives. He is right there with us as we suffer a moment of loneliness, each rejection and every separation.

His comfort is certain. *China Cry* reveals an intensely personal God, one who cares enough to reach down into the life of an obscure young Chinese girl who calls on Him in her hour of trial. And the message is clear. If Jesus stoops to deliver her from a personal hell on earth, won't He do the same for you? Won't he come into your world also?

Wherever you are on your own journey of faith, this is a story you will want to share with others and read over and over again.

—Dr. Paul F. Crouch, President
Trinity Broadcasting Network

FOREWORD

As daily news reports tell of massive shifts in geopolitics, we are facing an unprecedented era of new opportunity for the Gospel. And nowhere is this more true than in those lands once ominously known as "The Communist Bloc".

Here at Christian Broadcasting Network, we are preparing for the greatest harvest of souls in history. In the next years, we expect millions to be won to Christ from these once closed nations. And, thanks to faithful outreaches like Nora Lam ministries in San Jose, California, many of these millions will be Chinese.

Back in 1977, CBN began looking to the Far East—asking how we could better reach the world's 1.1 billion Chinese with the Gospel. Early on, the Lord blessed us with the discovery of a most remarkable woman of faith.

Meanwhile, presidents have come and gone in the USA. China has changed premiers. Yet Nora Lam has remained a tenacious ambassador for Christ to the Chinese people. Thanks to her God-given courage and faith, many closed doors have opened to the Gospel in spite of Marxist oppression.

In Nora Lam, we found not only a partner in ministry,

but a woman who has become a special friend of our family over the years that followed.

Dede and two of our children—Gordon and Anne— have even joined Nora on one of her many preaching missions to the Orient.

And we also discovered something else about Nora. Something that the late Kathryn Kuhlman recognized when she first asked Nora Lam to testify in her great healing crusades: *Nora's ministry is unique.* Her message cuts both ways —reaching out simultaneously to the West as well as the East.

God has anointed Nora Lam to serve as a "Gospel bridge" between China's millions and believers in the West.

Nora Lam has frequently been our guest on the 700 Club. Who will ever forget her appearance after the tragic violence of Tiananmen Square? With tears in her eyes, she shared her overwhelming burden for the Chinese people whom she loves so dearly. It is a love that many Americans have come to share with her over the years.

The Lord has also miraculously used her determined energy and unstoppable faith. I'll never forget one of my trips to China with Nora. At 4:00 in the morning I was awakened by noisy activity in the next room. It was Nora and her team, already up and working fervently!

Every Christian with a godly concern about the future needs to read this important volume. It will build your faith to attempt greater things for God as we enter into this new millennium of opportunity.

This new book reminds us once again that the miracle working power of God is still available to each one of us today. The Holy Spirit who delivered Nora from a communist firing squad is equipping believers for the future now.

Pat Robertson, President
Christian Broadcasting Network

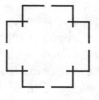

INTRODUCTION:

THE SEEDS HAVE BEEN PLANTED

I shall never forget him, the elderly missionary I met in 1967 whose death-bed prophecy came true.

It happened when my wife's mother was in the Parkway Terrace Nursing Home in Wheaton, Illinois. While visiting her we would chat with other residents. One of them was Pastor Grey, a frail little man in his late nineties. His skin was like pale parchment stretched over bone, his voice was weak, but his blue-gray eyes were bright with spirit.

I was intrigued to learn he had been a missionary in China most of his life. Yet I was saddened thinking that all his years in the Orient were for naught. For the news was full of Chairman Mao's Cultural Revolution when every vestige of Christianity in China appeared to be eliminated.

In my conversations with the missionary I avoided mention of this sadness but one day it was unavoidable. The latest bloodbath was making headlines and I couldn't help but comment: "I'm so sorry, but it looks like Christianity is pretty well wiped out in China."

His blue-gray eyes became electric and a thin hand reached over and took my arm. "Don't worry," he said in a voice which suddenly became strong. "Christianity will bloom in China. The seeds have been planted."

My elderly friend is now with the One he had served so well. But his words have become true. In 1990 we read that the largest Christian revival in China's history came out of the Cultural Revolution. And after the massacre at Tiananmen Square, the revival is spreading fast. "Students are converting to Christ at the rate of virtually a dorm a day," one student at Beijing's Beida University told News Network International.

But not until I came to know Nora Lam did I learn firsthand how those seeds came to be planted. Through her inspiring adventure with Jesus Christ, I found that no matter how strong and brutal the oppression, those seeds of faith had the power to germinate with the same tenacity of the wild-flower seed which forces its way up through a concrete pavement to meet the life-giving sun.

Today, Nora Lam and other dedicated Christians carry on that work in helping their countrymen and women meet the one true Jesus, Who can give the joy and fulfillment they so desperately seek.

Her life story of torture and tragedy, of romance and miracles, is an astounding saga you'll never forget.

DICK SCHNEIDER

A COLD WIND RISES

It was a beautiful Shanghai spring afternoon in 1953 when two classmates and I bicycled home from classes at Soochow University. A soft breeze drifted up from the Whangpoo River and with graduation only a few weeks away we girls laughed and talked about our futures. Suddenly, as we approached Bubbling Wells Road, our merriment froze.

An ominous-looking mob had gathered on the street ahead of us. From within the crowd erupted angry shouts and screams. We stared at each other, braked our bikes to a stop and walked them up to the crowd. We pushed our way through onlookers to see two young men beating an elderly man doubled up on the pavement. His smashed glasses lay next to him. One youth, lip curled, kicked him viciously in the stomach. The other slammed a stick across his face, screaming, "Evil-doer . . . poisonous snake!" Dark blood trickled from the old man's mouth.

Again my classmates and I looked at each other, our eyes wide. Had they caught a thief? A murderer?

A shrill voice split the air. We turned to see a girl in her late teens about my age, shouting at the crowd. "You see what happens to traitors who dare defy our glorious Republic!"

Suddenly, a horn blared stridently behind us and the onlookers gave way before a police car. I sighed with relief. At least the police would save the old man from further torture. No matter what he had done, no one deserved to suffer like this.

Two officers, shoving people aside, strode up to the two young men who turned to face them. Pointing to the old man, they said something to the policemen. They nodded, roughly picked up the unconscious victim like a sack of wheat, and dragged him to their squad car, the pavement pulling his slippers off his feet. After shoving him into the car, they roared off.

A small child scooped up the old man's slippers and raced away. I stood staring at the glass fragments of his spectacles, now mingled with blood, and felt myself becoming ill.

"What . . . what did he do?" I asked an older woman who was about to leave.

"Oh," she shrugged, "he was asking for it, the old fool."

"But what had he done wrong?" I pressed.

She stared at me for a moment, eyes shifting warily. Then she pulled herself together and, as if by rote, announced in a loud voice: "He was teaching the Christian Bible to young people. Everyone knows this is against the law." She looked around at the remaining crowd and continued: "Those stupid enough to believe in such fairy tales have no respect for our great leader, Chairman Mao."

The woman looked down at the spectacles and blood. "But no, there is always someone who wants to defy him." She glanced around, fear now in her eyes, and suddenly she left.

I turned to leave; with my stomach weak, I leaned heavily on my bike's handlebars.

"What's the matter, Neng Yee?" Chung Shin, one of my classmates, cried sardonically, "Can't stomach the cleansing of our republic?

"Or," she added sweetly, "is it because your fine father is a doctor and you're better than we proletariat?"

Anger and fear welled within me—anger at her false accusation, fear of what Chung Shin could do. I knew her too well. She was forever trying to wheedle herself into the Communist leaders' special favor. And I suspected one of her ways was to report "disloyalty" or other signs of subversion.

As a loyal Communist believer and Party worker, I feared nothing from this little frog who would sell herself for a Party leader's smile. Yet I knew how dangerous she could be. She was also jealous of my boyfriend, Cheng Shen. She often made eyes at him, but Cheng Shen, a quiet, studious man, never paid her any attention.

There was only one way to treat flies like Chung Shin. I looked into her eyes and smiled my sweetest smile. "How is it, Chung Shin, that I saw a Buddha in your mother's house? We all know that *all* religion is an opiate of the people."

Chung Shin's face turned the color of rice flour and she stared at me in fear. I let her squirm for a moment, then laughed: "Oh, I'm sure your mother has destroyed such things by now. Come," I grinned, "let's be on our way."

Climbing onto my bike I headed up Bubbling Well Road. I glanced at Chung Shin, her brows furrowed, quietly cycling beside me, and savored my revenge. I had learned my lessons well in this new regime. The only way to control people is through fear.

I waved goodbye to my classmates, who pedaled their separate ways and headed home deep in thought. I had struggled too hard to let anyone think they had gotten the better of me. This was a glorious new age in which we were living and I *would* come out on top. To this end I had studied like a scholar to soon gain a law degree, with high honors. I was fiercely proud of my country and vowed to serve it to the best of my ability. I had watched China suffer under the onslaught of the Japanese during World War II. I had studied the inspiring account of Mao Tse-tung's courageous Long March in 1934. I knew it had saved enough of our great Red Army, which helped realize his prophecy that "several hundred million peasants will rise like a mighty storm . . . they will sweep out the imperialists, warlords, corrupt officials, local tyrants, and evil gentry into their graves."

I glanced up at a red banner flapping in the wind above the street: "Never Forget Class Struggle." The same slogan surmounted our classrooms' doors. The message was even on our toothbrushes!

Yes, I knew of the many killings, such as the parasite landlords and other enemies of the people. But wasn't it Marx or Lenin who said a baby is birthed amid blood and pain? So wouldn't a new China be born amid bloodshed and struggle?

Chairman Mao had said, "Political power grows out of the barrel of a gun," and "Doing revolution is not like going to a tea party."

No, I grimaced as I pedaled, I did not expect a tea party. And as a lawyer for the state I looked forward to helping lead our revolution.

As I approached a dark boarded-up church, which was now being used as a machinery warehouse, I realized that of the many churches in Shanghai, only a few remained. And even these, I believed, would eventually die out. Now they were but a sop to those who still believed in such myths. Communism and Christianity could not exist together, we were instructed. Atheism, basic to communism, has no room for the supernatural, especially for folk tales, such as a man who died and came back to life again.

I remembered being taught such myths as a child in missionary school. As I passed the old church, I found myself, for some strange reason, humming, "Jesus Loves Me, this I know, for the Bible tells me so. . . ." A momentary poignancy touched me, but I bit my lip and chuckled. Yes, old habits die hard.

Even the habit of living comfortably, I thought wryly as I pedaled up in front of our "home." I stared at the crumbling bricks and broken window panes stuffed with rags and thought of the beautiful house in which Father, Mother, brother Neng Yao, and I used to live. Now our family was forced to live in one room in this hovel in which five other families also existed.

As I was about to pedal into the little dingy areaway, I stopped short, planted both feet on the ground, and stared. A new poster had been plastered on the wall since I had left this morning. It was like many others that appeared these days along Shanghai streets.

"Parasites must die!"

I knew it referred to my father. Deemed one of the intelligensia, he had long been under suspicion. In fact, he was already practically imprisoned in the hospital where he gave his all on behalf of the people.

I walked over to the poster, looked around to see if anyone was looking, and disdainfully ripped it down. The day would come when *I* would be in charge. And others would jump to my song.

As I stood there crumpling the poster in my hands, a cold chill seemed to come over me. Was it the rising wind . . . or something else? I straightened my shoulders and lifted my head. Neng Yee was tough. Anyone who had gone through the terrible ordeals I survived *had* to be strong. Even so, as I thought about that terrible day it all started, I shuddered.

2

TERROR BY DAY

A terrible thing happened.

My best friend had disappeared. I raced from room to room as fast as my seven-year-old legs could carry me crying: "Shirley! Shirley!" I rushed into the living room with its silken drapes; she wasn't there. I looked into the dining room with its black-lacquered furniture. Panic-stricken I clattered up the white marble stairs crying for my mother.

She had already started down the steps, and we met halfway on the stairway. "Dear Neng Yee," she soothed, bending down and placing her arms around me. "What *is* the matter?"

"Oh Mommy, Mommy, Shirley is gone. I can't find her anywhere!"

My governess, puffing with exertion, came up the stairs to us. "Oh, Madame Neng, we've looked everywhere, and she's not to be found."

Mother wiped my tears away with a white linen handkerchief. "There, there, my child, don't cry," she soothed. She was pensive for a moment, forefinger on her chin.

"Didn't you take her with you yesterday when we visited the Ying family?"

I stopped crying, realization dawning on me.

"Oh yes, Mommy, yes! I left her there." And then I began sobbing more than ever.

"Oh, she will be lost forever. She'll be stolen, kidnapped. I'll never see my poor Shirley again!"

"My little lotus blossom," Mother said, patting my head, "don't cry." She signaled to one of the servants. "Call the Yings." As the servant picked up the phone, Mother said, "Now, now, Neng Yee, a rickshaw man will bring Shirley here very shortly."

"Oh thank you, Mommy," I sniffled, hugging her. "I love you more than ever!"

Mother kissed me good-bye as she was on her way out to play mah-jongg with friends; I went out our entrance door with her to wait for the rickshaw man. Our black Mercedes gleaming in the bright sunshine, waited in the driveway, its chauffeur standing at attention at the passenger door. Seeing mother, he bowed and pulled the door open for her. As I watched I was so proud of mother, so gracious and petite. She blew me a kiss from the window, and the limousine purred away through the gate.

I stood in front of our sprawling estate on the outskirts of Shanghai awaiting the return of my beloved friend. My governess and maid stood with me.

Soon I heard the slap-slap of sandals as the rickshaw man trotted up our tree-lined drive. Seeing us, he grinned and looked back into his cab. Yes, my Shirley Temple doll was there, safe amidst silken pillows.

I almost swooned with relief. As soon as the rickshaw stopped, my governess scooped up the doll and placed her in my outstretched arms. She paid the driver who glanced at the doll, then at me and smiled. For Shirley and I were both dressed alike, ruffled skirt and starched petticoats, shiny black patent leather Mary Jane shoes. But Shirley's hair was blond and curly; mine was straight and black. While the governess collected the pillows, I examined my friend and then held her up before me.

"Her shoes," I ordered, solemnly imitating my mother's tone when she addressed the household help.

Obediently, my governess dusted the doll's shoes with her sleeve, then dropped to her knees and wiped my shoes. I waited with the calm assurance of a princess until she finished.

A bit bored now that my fright was over, I walked out into our garden, followed by my usual retinue which, in addition to the governess and maid, included my tutor and our gardener.

Suddenly, turning around to face them, I ordered them to play Follow-the-Leader. Carefully placing Shirley on the grass, I bent down and performed a somersault, unmindful of the green grass stains that appeared on my white dress. I chortled with glee as my chubby governess attempted the same maneuver, her wide face crimson with exertion. The maid, a younger thin girl managed fairly well. The tutor tried and failed. Our gardener, an older man, pleaded he was unable to do it.

I was about to demand he follow my orders when a roar shattered the sky. The women screamed in terror, and we craned our necks to see a silver airplane bearing red circles on its wings flash past above the trees.

"Japanese!" shouted the gardener, his eyes wide with fright.

I had heard my parents and their friends talk in hushed tones about the "enemy." The Japanese, it seemed, had invaded our land several years ago. And though our brave soldiers fought valiantly, they were slowly being pushed back and now the Japanese were taking over the capitol city of Shanghai.

Grumph! Grumph! The ground shuddered under my feet to be followed by the heavy thud of distant thunder. Only the sky was still blue.

"They are bombing," screamed my governess. She picked me up and raced for the house. I dropped my doll and screamed, "Shirley! Shirley!" Inside the house, the governess put me down, and I cried for Shirley.

"Don't let her be hurt!"

The governess turned to the maid and pointed at the door. Pale with fear, the girl ran out on the lawn, picked up the doll, and stumbled back into the house, panting heavily.

I did not know it then but my life would never be the same.

That evening at dinner with Father home from his medical practice, the afternoon's terror seemed like a bad dream. Surely, nothing could harm this pleasant life we enjoyed. Father sat at the head of the table in his Western-style suit. The maid served him another helping of fatted pork, his favorite dish.

"Ummmm," he smiled, "please convey my gratitude to the chef."

She bowed and brought the dish to Mother who smiled, shook her head, and pointed to the boiled crab dish she so loved. Mother was so careful not to offend anyone, not even the maids. I believed it was because she, too, had loving parents. She had told me her father was a prosperous merchant who was a trader of seafood with Japan, and that she had been educated in both Chinese and American schools.

I loved looking at her, so tiny, she was not even five feet tall. Tonight she looked so beautiful in her shimmering silk gown, her pale green jade necklace gleaming in the glow of candles.

My Shirley Temple doll sat at the table across from me in her own chair. I insisted the maid serve her a helping, too.

Mother glanced at father waiting for direction in the conversation. But our usual lively table talk was muted.

After lifting another morsel of fatted pork to his lips with chopsticks, Father muttered to himself: "I'll pay ten dollars for every Chinese soldier you can find in Shanghai tonight." Then he glanced at Mother.

"No panic," he reassured her. "They will need doctors but the servants should be released."

"I mentioned it this morning," said Mother. "They refuse to go."

I stared at my plate. I didn't want to hear about ugly things like the war. I would rather Father talk of happy things, such as when he was a youth. I loved to listen to his stories about when he studied in France. He had travelled there at the age of thirteen and remained there until he graduated from the University of Lyon with a medical degree.

I always enjoyed hearing him tell of having coffee on that boulevard with the wonderful-sounding name, Champs Elysees, and how he climbed the Eiffel Tower. But the French seemed to be such unusual people; they ate strange foods in an odd way, using sharp metal implements.

As I lifted rice with my chopsticks, I thought how clumsy and noisy it must be to eat with such heavy, sharp things.

One good thing about this evening, however, was that father was feeling better than usual. He suffered from asthma and bronchitis, and during the winter he coughed a lot. I would wince when I heard him; it sounded so painful.

My cantankerous step-grandmother was responsible for this, I knew. Mother had confided in me that, when Father was a little boy, he lived with her in the country, and she was very cruel. "She never allowed him enough clothing to keep warm during the cold winter months," she said sadly. "That is why he went to France so young," she added, "to escape her tyranny."

Even then I did not like my step-grandmother and feared the thought of being in her presence. I became depressed thinking of her.

I would rather hear about my grandfather. When my parents spoke of him their eyes brightened. Sung Han Cheng seemed to be a good and wise man who was chairman of the board of the Bank of China. Father said he lived in Chungking.

"Where is Chungking?" I asked.

"Far, far away, my little princess," smiled Father. "It will be our country's capital now that our city has been taken by the enemy. It is far west of here—some fifteen hundred miles, so far away that the Japanese soldiers will never reach it."

We never received any letters from him, and I now understood why. Chungking seemed as far away as the moon. I knew I would never travel that far, but oh, how I would like to meet my grandfather. He seemed so kind and nice compared to my step-grandmother.

But as weeks went on I did not need visions of this mean-spirited woman to make me feel bad.

The gloom that settled in our house deepened as the war went on. It brightened only when my parents' friends visited our house to play mah-jongg. Then amidst the clicking of ivory tiles, I would hear them call out such expressions as:

"Four bam."

"Six dot."

"Flower."

"North."

"Three dot."

"One bam."

"Five crack."

"South."

Later, when I asked Father about this game, he explained it was thousands of years old. "It is also called 'The

Game of the Four Winds,' " he said, "but it is not so engross-
ing that you can't have good conversation with your friends
while playing it." Winking, he patted me on the head.

"When you're old enough I'll teach you how to play
it."

But such happy evenings happened less and less. More
and more Mother and Father talked in hushed tones of things
I didn't understand. They spoke of the enemy forcing foreign
missionaries into concentration camps.

Some nights I would see them leave carrying clothes
and food, looking very serious. Usually when they went out
they were laughing and happy. Then my governess told me
they were taking necessary items to the foreign missionaries
who were starving.

"They put themselves in danger doing this," sighed
my governess. She closed her eyes and rocked back and forth
half-singing to herself, "May Buddha protect them, may Buddha protect them."

But the god she spoke of certainly did not protect my
parents' finances. I overheard them talk of the Chinese stock
market crashing, of losing their American investments.

One night Father sadly told of a businessman friend
who was so despondent over losing all his money he hung
himself in the family garage.

"But there is no reason for anyone to do such a thing
as that," he said. "No reason." Father was brought up in the
Catholic faith in France, and he said suicide was a "mortal
sin." I didn't know what that was but it sounded ominous. He
did not go to church regularly, but I understood that his reluc-
tance to eat meat on Friday—even his beloved fatted pork—
was part of his Catholic upbringing.

What seemed more important to Mother and Father
was that our country's money had lost its value with the Japanese invasion. I heard them talking in low tones about this in
the library and heard such words as *penniless* and *poor*.

But it wasn't the thought of being poor that chilled me. It was what the enemy soldiers seemed to be doing to our people. I heard our household help whispering of men being bayoneted on the street, or hung from telephone poles with their bodies dangling until they rotted. A maid tearfully told my governess how she was rudely stopped a few days early by a soldier who stripped her of her watch and rings. She started to say something else, but she saw me listening and said: "But it could have been worse."

I turned to my doll. "Shirley, you will be safe with me. No bad men will ever come into *this* house."

But one day they did.

It was a quiet Sunday afternoon. Father was reading, Mother was embroidering, and I was arranging little China plates so Shirley and I could have a tea party.

Suddenly, Father raised his head. "What is that?" he asked.

Then we heard it, the groaning of heavy trucks coming up our driveway. Loud pounding shook our door. A maid hurried to open it. It was thrown back roughly and a Japanese officer strode arrogantly into the room. Soldiers carrying rifles with bayonets stood behind him.

Mother's hands flew to her mouth, Father rose to his feet.

"You have six hours to be out of here," the officer shouted. "This house is being taken over on behalf of the Imperial Government of Japan!"

Mother cried out; Father stepped to her side, his arm around her. I rushed to them and buried my face in Mother's gown.

The next six hours were a nightmare. We were told we could take only what we could carry. I stared hopelessly at my closets full of clothes, my many shoes, my toys. "Mommy," I cried, "how can we carry all of them?"

Mother drew me to her and looked around at her

beautiful drapes, the handsome furniture, at the maids who were helping her pack the few suitcases we would carry.

"Sweetheart," she said, "you must learn that such things are not important to us now. What is important is that we still have each other."

I did not quite understand what Mother meant, but before the day was over I knew that my life as a princess was over.

Six hours later, Mother, Father, and I walked out of our front door carrying our suitcases. The household help had lined up to say good-bye. Tears streamed down their faces; my governess kneeled down and pulled me close to her. "Oh good-bye, my little princess, keep well. I shall miss you."

The Japanese officer, his men standing impassively behind him, watched us, his hands on his hips.

Our chauffeur had the Mercedes in the driveway, motor idling. He opened the rear door for us. A soldier viciously kicked the door shut and slammed his rifle butt into the chauffeur's face.

He fell back against the car, eyes wide in astonishment, blood streaming from his jaw. Mother screamed. Father shushed her. I clutched Shirley close and buried my face in her dress.

"Down with the suitcases!" ordered the officer. My parents looked at him, puzzled.

"Open them!" he ordered. They did and three soldiers tore through the contents. One found Mother's jewelry—her jade necklace and a gold bracelet. He held them up triumphantly. Another pulled a gold pocket watch out of Father's suitcase. Then the officer stepped up to Mother and grabbed her hand on which her diamond ring sparkled in the sunlight. Mother's face creased with pain as he roughly pulled it off her finger. Father stood impassive, but I could see his hands trembling. They took his wristwatch, then the officer pointed to the street. "Go!"

Behind us soldiers began pasting up long strips of yellow paper with Japanese characters on them, sealing our doors and windows.

"Come, Neng Yee," said Father motioning to me. We picked up our small suitcases and began walking down the tree-lined driveway. My governess cried out as we walked away. I turned to see a soldier force her to the ground with the point of his gleaming bayonet pressed to her neck.

Father pulled me around.

Screams and rifle fire crackled behind us.

"We must keep walking, Neng Yee," he said, his voice tight. "Don't look back."

We trudged along the street for a long time, Mother and Father not saying anything. The street was unnaturally quiet. Occasionally a frightened-looking rickshaw man passed us, head down, slap-slapping down the street. In the distance, a Japanese army truck full of soldiers swung around a corner.

"Mother," I whimpered, "where are we going?"

She compressed her lips and for a long time said nothing. Then, as if each word pained her to say it, she sighed· "To your step-grandmother's house. We have no other place to go."

3

HORROR BY NIGHT

The sun had disappeared when we finally trudged into the French section of Shanghai, which as yet was somewhat free of enemy persecution. A cold fall wind, rank with the smell of the Yangtze River, blew in our faces, and Father coughed. Still, trembling with fear and clutching Shirley, I kept peering over my shoulder at shadows, expecting an enemy soldier to leap out at us.

Father and Mother were quiet and only the scrape of our shoes on the cobblestones broke the silence. Then after what seemed like hours of walking, Father stopped and pointed. "There," he said in a low tone.

Something cold clutched my heart as I looked at the big, gray house. Looming against the darkening sky, it seemed to personify the meanness and evil of the woman who held dominion over it. The ancient three-story structure leaned on what appeared to be a newer addition.

Father's shoulders sagged as we stood looking at it. Then, he motioned us through the wrought-iron gate into the courtyard. "Come, let us get it over with."

He tugged a rusting bell chain. Finally a dim light

glimmered behind the frosted window. The door creaked open, and the frightened face of a maid peeped out at us.

"It's Han Tsin, and his family," said Father.

The maid disappeared, the door closed, and we waited some minutes. Then I heard it, a sound I would soon both hate and fear, a distant cackling that grew louder.

The door was opened by the maid; behind her stood a wizened woman, her gray hair pulled back in a bun. She had tiny eyes that gleamed with malice and glee.

"Ah, ah!" she cackled, her arms folded before her, "so my ungrateful stepson has finally decided to pay his poor old ancestress a visit." Her eyes darted at mother and me. "And he has brought his brood with him."

Father bowed and said quietly. "We have no place to go. The enemy took our home."

Our suitcases made that obvious, but Grandmother relished twisting the knife, even though I felt sure she had known earlier in the day we were on our way.

"Ho, ho," she chortled, "and now he and his ungrateful wife and," her eyes seemed to pierce me, "brat of a child want to live off of me."

Father had evidently expected this reception and waited patiently until his stepmother had her fill.

Then we walked into the house, Grandmother taking small hobbling steps. I gasped when I saw the reason. She had bound feet; they were only about three inches long! I had heard this was done in ancient times, but then, I thought, Grandmother was very old, too.

As we passed through darkened rooms of the newer part of the house, I heard giggling in the shadows. From them several children about my age peeked at us.

"Look how ugly she is," one whispered. "And that doll," hissed another, "I shall smash it my first chance!"

I gripped Mother's hand and pulled Shirley closer to me.

Then we stepped into a hall I shall never forget. It was the main floor of the old house, and my nostrils stung with an overpowering rank odor. As my eyes became accustomed to the dark, I saw the source of the smell. Slabs of drying, salted meat hung from the rafters. I couldn't help but think of the decaying bodies hanging from telephone poles along Shanghai streets.

My stomach sickened, and I averted my eyes from the blackened chunks only to shrink from another frightening scene. Rows of Buddha statues stared at me, their glass eyes glinting in the dim light.

Grandmother saw me recoil and laughed: "They will watch you night and day, my child." Her bony hand clutched my shoulder. "They will tell me *everything* you do. So don't think you can get away with anything in *this* house."

I cringed as I walked by her gods of clay and stone. And when Grandmother led us to a flight of stairs saying, "You all will live on the second floor," I was relieved to not be close to her idols.

"No one's lived on the second or third floor for years," she cackled, "so you'll have to get used to a little dust."

A "little" was an understatement. When she showed us the one room and bath in which we would live, Mother gave a little gasp. Cobwebs festooned the corners, and grime was everywhere. I didn't even want to walk into it.

However, after Grandmother hobbled down the steps, Mother took a rag and began brushing away the cobwebs. "Tomorrow," she told Father, "I'll get some soap and water and do some real cleaning."

I helped her. It was the first time in my life I had done any real work with my hands. Only there was not much work, for the room contained only a bed and dresser for my parents and a long box on which I would sleep. A chair at the end of it provided room for my legs and feet. The other rooms on the second and third floor were closed off, and I didn't dare look into them. Who knew? Perhaps a giant Buddha lived in one of them.

When I asked Mother about these strange gods she explained that Buddhism was an ancient religion, common to many Middle Eastern countries, and was based on the life of a mortal man who was born in 563 B.C. and died at the age of eighty.

"They say he became very wise and holy and was called Buddha, meaning the 'awakened or enlightened one.' "

Mother went on to say that a wise old scholar once told her how the Buddha religion came to China. He said that two thousand years ago when Jesus Christ was born, the emperor of China saw a great light. He knew that a most Holy One had been born so he sent out his scholars to search the world for Him.

Mother put her hand over her mouth to smother a smile. "I shouldn't make light of this," she said, "but the story goes that the emperor's scholars did not search well enough. And when they came across followers of Buddha, they assumed *he* was the Holy One and so they brought Buddhism back to China.

"It has become a very complicated religion," she added, "and his followers have many rules for living. There are many different sects who have different ways."

She stopped for a moment, shook her head and made a wry face. "But Father's stepmother has her *own* way of worshiping Buddha."

And Grandmother did have strange ways regarding him. She would daily ask her statues if anyone had stolen anything. She must have believed they answered her, for she was constantly accusing one of her servants of wrongdoing. From morning to night her cracked angry voice filled the house.

She seemed only to have an affection for her two daughters and their children who lived with her in the new addition. And it was these girls who made my life particularly miserable.

They never entered our dank wing of the house, and when I'd meet one in the new addition she would turn her back.

One day I approached a cousin about my age and held out my Shirley doll. "Hello, would you like to meet my Shirley Temple?" I asked.

She narrowed her eyes, pointed a finger at me, and snarled, "Wild seed from hell. Stay away from us!"

As she fled laughing down the hall I stood riveted in shock. *What* was she talking about?

I put her angry accusation in the back of my mind, for my parents had recently enrolled me in an elementary school near Grandmother's house. It was called the McTyier Christian School. I looked forward to it.

The classes were interesting. But what really intrigued me was when my teacher told us about a Holy Man named Jesus. At first I wondered if she was talking about someone like Buddha. But then she said Jesus was the Son of the One Who created the world and all of us, that God had sent Him down to earth to teach us how to live. When she described how He was killed, came back to life again, and now lived in the world today, though no one could see Him, I knew this was no Buddha.

Still, it all was difficult for me to comprehend. But I enjoyed singing the hymns and hearing the missionaries tell how this Jesus loved little children.

"He wants to be your friend," my teacher told me. Such a friend would be wonderful, I thought, especially during the lonely, scary times. At night before going to sleep in my box bed, I would pretend to talk to my invisible Friend. But it wasn't much different than talking to Shirley. At least she was a friend I could see.

I at least had made new friends at school. But then

they became cool toward me. I wondered what had changed them and then discovered my cousins had been telling them stories about me.

"Your cousin said you were a 'wild seed,' " one of the children said to me as we stood out on the school grounds. "She said your Mother and Father are not your real parents, that you were an unwanted child who had been abandoned in a hospital.

"Tell me," she pressed, "is it true?"

I could only stare at her, shaking my head. Bursting into tears I raced home. I found Mother in our little bedroom pensively looking at some photographs she had packed in her suitcase that day we left home.

Sobbing, I threw myself on her lap and told her about my schoolmate's charge.

Mother gathered me in her arms and was silent for a long time. Then she sighed: "It is time for you to know."

I looked up, her gentle face was full of love, and tears brimmed in her brown eyes.

"You were born . . . in the Wee Yo Hospital, an old missionary hospital, in Peking in 1932," she said, her voice catching. "Your mother was a young girl in love with a handsome opera singer. She was well educated, very beautiful, and from a high, famous family. Your real father was also highly educated and very handsome. The two were very much in love."

I listened, enchanted at what sounded like a sad but beautiful fairy tale, but one I knew was true.

"But in China," Mother continued, "one must marry within his or her own class. And your real mother was from a higher class than her lover. Her parents would not consent to their marriage despite your father's talent. So your mother had no choice but to leave her precious baby in the hospital."

Tears warmed my cheeks as I thought of the sad, young mother.

"My cousin, Dr. Soo," mother went on, "was an intern in the hospital when you were born. She knew your father and I had been married for many years and were unable to have any children of our own. Since you were such a lovely baby, she thought we might want you. So she wrote and sent us your picture."

I held my breath, hoping the mother who held me would take me.

"The minute I saw your beautiful picture, I knew you were meant for me. Your father knew it, too. We immediately asked Dr. Soo to hire a nanny until you were old enough to travel. When you were just six months old, your nanny brought you to our house to live forever."

I had never felt happier. I was sad for the poor young girl who had to give me up. But I was overjoyed that Mother and Father had wanted me so much.

"Oh, Mother," I cried, "I'm so glad you adopted me! I will try to be a good girl so everybody will respect our family."

Then Mother opened her bureau drawer and took out a beautiful little black silk evening purse. On one side glowed an opal surrounded by tiny sparkling diamonds. Opening it she took out two photos of me taken when I was only seven days old. There was also a folded paper giving details of my birth and adoption.

As Mother looked at my picture, a gentle smile on her face, I felt even more loved—and important.

The taunting of my cousins didn't bother me anymore. I found them easy to ignore. And soon my schoolmates seemed to have forgotten my cousins' accusations.

I realized blood relationship was most important to my cousins. But from what I was learning at missionary school, and the care of my adoptive parents, I knew that love was far more important than blood. It was the most important thing of all.

But if love was lacking anywhere, it was most absent in the dark house of my step-grandmother. From what little I knew of the Buddhist religion, I knew that compassion for others was one of its tenets. But Grandmother seemed to have her own ideas. For example, she always polished her plate at mealtimes because she said Buddha told her that for every clean plate she could buy another acre of land.

If Buddha was right, I knew I would never own as much as a cup of Chinese soil. For I hardly ever left my plate clean. Since my parents had no kitchen and were usually gone at mealtimes, I had to eat with Grandmother and her family. My small portion was usually leftovers and scraps, some of which I could not stomach.

Once she took delight in dropping an ugly wrinkled skin of a duck's neck on my plate.

"If you don't eat it," she warned, "I will have Buddha pierce you with his chopsticks and pull out your hair, thread by thread."

My cousins gloated at my discomfort. Finally, I slowly stuffed the greasy skin into my mouth but couldn't get it down. Gagging and retching, I fled the table with the raucous laughter of my cousins following me. I often went to bed hungry and didn't dare tell my parents because I didn't want to worry them.

Father came home so haggard from his medical practice, now under Japanese jurisdiction. He was coughing a lot, and the clammy air in Grandmother's house didn't help his asthma and bronchitis. Mother was so very busy helping other people. The enemy occupation made it even more imperative that people band together for survival.

Even so, Mother and Father were able to eke out a small social life, which seemed necessary for them to be able to face the next day. Often they would be out late at night. Thus I spent many hours crying with loneliness and fear in the frightening old wing of Grandmother's house.

Sometimes I would sneak over to the maid's room above the garage and crawl into bed with her until my parents came home. When I heard them knock on the garage door for the maid to unlock the huge wrought-iron gate in the courtyard, I'd race down the back stairs, tear across the cold, cobbled courtyard with its wind-rippled fishpond reflecting eerie shadows, slip into the old wing, scurry past the stinking slabs of meat, rush up the stairway, and dive into my cold bed. When my parents would come in I'd pretend to be asleep.

But the horror of night was more than matched by the terror in the streets by day. Starving people stood shivering in long lines for meager rice rations, and the enemy soldiers seemed to have lost all restraint. A young boy was shot because he was wearing a Boy Scout uniform.

On the way home from school I saw three soldiers order an old rickshaw man to carry them. When he protested that three were too heavy, one slammed a rifle butt into his stomach.

He folded into a heap on the street, and when they ordered him to get up he could only move one hand limply. One of the soldiers then simply sunk his bayonet into the old man's side.

I muffled a scream, turned and ran home like a frightened mouse. I felt sure they were chasing me. As I hammered on our front door, no one would answer. Finally, a cousin peered through the window, stuck out her tongue, and yelled, "Go to the rear door!"

In panic, I stumbled to the back where another cousin, laughing with glee, ordered me to the front door. Back and forth I ran, crazed with fear, until tiring of the game, a cousin let me in.

This happened every afternoon. Each time I'd cringe past my taunting cousins, clatter up the stairs to our room, and bury my face in the folds of my mother's fleecy red bathrobe and sob.

On one such terrible afternoon, I stumbled into our room completely hopeless. Mother and Father were gone, my Shirley Temple doll was of no solace, and I flung myself on the bed burying my face in Mother's pillow.

"O God, help me!" I found myself crying. "O God, help me!"

I don't know how long I laid there pleading for help, but suddenly I had the feeling that someone was in the room with me.

Turning my head and opening my eyes, I saw an ancient Chinese man standing inside the closed door. He was smiling at me. *How did he get in?* I wondered. The door had been closed; I had not heard it open nor a footstep.

I sat up in bed. Perhaps he was a new servant, I thought. He wore a servant's clothing, a long blue overshirt that brushed the floor. He was so old looking, yet his kindly wrinkled face was full of love. His hair and long beard were pure white.

"Don't be afraid," he said softly in the Mandarin dialect. "I come from God." He pointed a thin finger upward.

"Sung Neng Yee," he said gently, calling me by my full Chinese name, "you have prayed to God, and He has heard you. He has sent me to be your friend, to comfort and help you."

4

HEARTBREAK STATION

I bolted upright on my cot and stared at the old man, my heart pounding. He seemed real, and then, not real. But strangely I was not afraid.

"You don't need to cry because of the way your cousins treat you," he said.

How did he know they were troubling me?

"I'll be your friend," he smiled.

I snatched up my doll and hugged her. "Shirley! Shirley!" I cried. "Did you hear? The new God is real. He has heard my prayer and sent us a friend!"

I jumped off the cot in joy. And then a thought chilled me. What if he went away as mysteriously as he came and never returned?

"Promise you'll come whenever I need you?" I begged.

He nodded. And then he was gone.

I couldn't wait to tell Mother when she came home. After listening carefully, she looked at me quizzically.

"No Mother," I pressed, "I'm not making it up. He came. *He came. He's real.*"

She smiled, drew me to her and said: "I'd love to meet him, Neng Yee. Would you invite him here, right now?"

I stared at her for a moment and sensed he wouldn't come unless I was alone.

"Oh . . . uh, I'm sorry, Mother, but . . ."

She seemed to understand and hugged me. "That's all right, my lotus blossom; let him come as he will."

That night when my parents thought I was asleep, I heard them discussing my mysterious visitor. "You know, children often create make-believe friends," said Father, quietly. "A pediatrician friend told me such a thing can fill a child's need. Even though she is eleven, Neng Yee's old man could be a good thing for her."

I smiled. No matter what they thought, I knew my friend was real.

From then on he came to see me almost every afternoon, standing inside the door, in the same long blue overshirt, with the same benevolent smile on his face. And I basked in the same warm peace he brought with him.

If he was make-believe as father thought, then how could he tell me such things that were so useful to the family, such as the best time to get in line for our family's rice ration?

After a few such experiences, Mother, I feel, began to believe he was real. "You know, I have heard of such beings," she said with a touch of awe, "they are called angels." She was thoughtful for a moment. "Perhaps he is your guardian angel."

I asked the old man when next he came. "Are you an angel?"

"Yes," he said gently, "your mother was right."

"And are you my guardian angel?" He smiled gently. And I knew it was so.

Then one day he brought the most wonderful news.

"You and your family are going to escape from Shanghai and this house," he said. "You will travel a long, hard journey. But you will reach a faraway city and meet your grandfather."

I was thrilled. I knew Grandfather was in faraway Chungking, which had not been captured by the Japanese. But how would we be able to go there? The Japanese would never allow us to leave. I looked up to ask the old man but he was gone.

When Mother and Father returned, I could hardly wait to give them the news. Father was dumbfounded at first, and then he slowly shook his head. "To live in Chungking would be to live in freedom," he sighed. "But *that* would take a miracle."

Mother gently took me by the shoulders and from her face I could tell she believed. "Call the old man back, Neng Yee," she begged, "and ask him *how* it will happen."

I waited until they had left the house the next day, kneeled down at my cot as we were taught in missionary school and prayed, asking God to send His angel. In a few minutes he was standing inside the door.

"Please, my friend," I said . . .

"Yes," he nodded, smiling, "your mother and father want to know all details—exactly how and . . . when?"

"Yes, yes," I exclaimed, standing on one foot, then the other.

"Tell them in about one week," he said, "there will be a knock on the door. A messenger will come and instruct them exactly what to do."

He vanished. When I told my parents, Father was still a bit dubious, but I noticed Mother began carefully going through what little belongings we had left. "Some we'll take," she said quietly, "most we will leave."

A week later Grandmother banged on our door. Her shriveled face was puzzled and suspicious.

"There is a man downstairs who wants to see you," she told my father.

He gave us a surprised look, then said to Grandmother, "Tell him to come up."

She was obviously disappointed for she would not be able to hear what the visit was all about.

A middle-aged stranger stepped into our room. There was a confident, serious air about him. After making sure no one stood outside our door, he closed it, sat down on a chair Father offered him, and began talking.

Looking at my father, he said: "Your father has sent me as his agent to bring you and your family to Chungking."

Father glanced at us in surprise, and Mother took my hand. I could feel her trembling.

"As you know," the stranger continued, "it will be a trip of about fifteen hundred miles. Our transportation will be uncertain, and we will have to walk part of the way. Because we'll have to avoid Japanese soldiers, we will make our way through forests and climb mountains. There will be many weeks of ordeal before we can even think of crossing into free China."

It sounded so exciting, I picked up my doll and hugged her.

"The trip will be dangerous, and you must not breathe a word about our destination," he added. Then a shadow crossed his face. "Some of us may die on the way. But those who make it will be able to live in freedom once again, with food to eat."

I was so happy that the old man's words were coming true, that I exclaimed: "Shirley, did you hear that? The trip will be hard, but we will make it because the old man told me so."

"I'm sorry," said the secret agent, sadly shaking his head. "But the child will have to leave her doll behind. You must all travel as beggars so no one will suspect you are escaping to Chungking." He glanced at me sympathetically. "A beggar would not have such a doll."

I stared at mother expecting her to object. But she sadly nodded. "He is right, Neng Yee."

After the secret agent left, I broke into bitter tears. Then, as I reconciled myself to leaving my doll, I began seeking places to hide her so my cousins wouldn't find her. I could see them playing roughly with her, or worse, even twisting off her head.

Disguised as beggars sounded exciting. But when Mother brought in the dirty, ragged garments I would have to wear, I blanched. "Ugh, mother," I sniffed, "must I really wear those awful rags?"

"Yes," she said, "and you will also have dirt smeared on your face."

My eyes widened, and I began to object; mother shushed me. "It is a small price to pay for freedom, Neng Yee."

I felt a little better when I saw the long beggar's dresses with the thick quilted padding inside that Mother and I would wear. At least they would be warm. Then, when she disheveled her hair to complete the disguise, I giggled. Mother who was so careful of her beautiful coiffure and peach-like complexion was now working hard to look repulsive.

Later, I would be glad she did.

On the morning we were to leave, Father brought us a container of wet mud. "Don't worry," he smiled, "I tried to find the cleanest dirt."

As we smeared our faces and hands, I decided it was a small price to pay for escaping Grandmother, my cousins and the dark old house that had been a prison for me.

As we walked out into the courtyard, a brisk late fall breeze ruffled our garments. I felt excited and happy about our trip. Grandmother stood at the door and pressed Father as to where we were going.

"It is time," he said, "that we stopped imposing on

you." It was all he could say. As he bid her good-bye, did I actually see disappointment in her wizened eyes? Perhaps, I thought wickedly, she will miss having someone to scream at.

As it was, she hobbled with us to the gate and said something to Father I couldn't catch. He seemed touched, bent down, and kissed her wrinkled cheek.

Perhaps it was because of his kind gesture. But I did something that surprised me. I had carried my doll, planning to give it to one of the many children now wandering the streets.

My cousins stood behind Grandmother watching us. None said anything, nor could I see anger or hate in their eyes. Obviously, they were surprised by our departure and didn't know what to make of it. On impulse, I walked up to the cousin who had taunted me the most and handed her Shirley.

"Here," I said, "she will be a good friend; maybe you'll come to love her as I did."

My cousin stood open-mouthed, holding the doll. Then in a thin voice she choked, "Thank you, Neng Yee."

It was the first time a cousin had spoken my name. My eyes misted, and I quickly turned my head. Too bad, I thought as I walked away, we could have been friends.

The gate closed behind us and we became simply three beggars amid the welter of humanity thronging the street. My disguise was soon tested when a schoolmate approached and glanced at me in pity, showing no sign of recognition.

We reached the railroad station where we would board the train for Nanking, the first stage of our journey. Any thoughts I may have had about leaving my home for the last three years were lost in the clamor and confusion of the smoky terminal.

Thousands of people jammed the place, pushing and

shouting. Our guide met us, glanced approvingly at our clothes, and told us to wait near a certain track.

"The train to Nanking will arrive shortly," he said. Measuring the crowd, he added: "You'll have to fight your way on board." He shook hands with Father. "I will meet you in Nanking." And then he disappeared.

As we waited amid the clamoring throng, I looked at my parents. In Father's eyes I could see his sorrowful resignation at leaving all of his property behind him. In Mother's, I could see her regret at parting from her friends and the mahjongg games she so much enjoyed. As for me, I was still excited. It even felt good to be among such crowds; it had been so long since I had seen so many human beings together.

A hoarse shriek split the air as our train pulled into the station, its grimy locomotive hissing and panting, snorting steam from its cylinders. Even before it groaned to a stop, the crowd exploded into a maelstrom of screaming, clawing savages, fighting to board the coaches. It was obvious this train could only take a fraction of the waiting people.

I was caught up in the struggling avalanche like a branch in a rushing stream. I lost sight of my parents; all I could see were flailing arms and churning legs. Petrified with fear, I cried out, "Oh God, please help me! Don't let them leave without me. God, please help!"

Suddenly, there were my parents standing on the edge of the crowd beckoning me.

"Mother! Mother!" I screamed, running to them. As I clung to Mother's long ragged dress, tears washed trails through the mud on my cheeks. Sobbing with relief, I knew even more surely that God heard my cry; He was truly alive.

Father guided us through the bedlam to a coach door and helped us up the steel steps. He pushed into the people-packed interior motioning us to follow. The car was so jammed it was impossible for anyone to fall down as the train lurched out of the station.

Under the hot sun, our coach became a pressure cooker of humanity. Father said the trip would take eight hours, and even before we left the outskirts of Shanghai I didn't think I could stand another ten minutes. I clung to mother as the train swayed and bumped, click-clacking along the rails. The smell of bodies mingled with the rising odor of sweat, urine, and vomit was making me sick. As the hours passed no one could reach the restrooms; people couldn't help but relieve themselves where they stood.

An older woman next to me moaned and collapsed. But the crush was so great she could only sag as her family tried to fan her. As the heat and stench increased, so did my nausea. Not wanting to throw up amidst all these people, I shut my eyes and concentrated on the click-clacking of the wheels as the hours passed.

For a long time I seemed to have slipped into a merciful limbo, then I was brought to reality by an increasing murmur of voices filling the coach. The click-clacking was slowing; Father reached down and touched my shoulder. "We're coming into Nanking," he said.

As our train shuddered to a stop, the murmurs became loud wailing.

"What is it?" I asked. My parents' faces had seemingly turned to stone and they wouldn't answer. I squeezed my way to a window. Lining the station platform in the late afternoon sun were lines of Japanese soldiers in mustard-colored uniforms. But it was the fiendish expressions on their faces that struck terror through me. They all looked like hungry cats who had just caught a mouse.

5

LONG MARCH

I shuddered, remembering the words of our guide back in Shanghai: "Some of us may even die on the way."

Now I didn't want to leave the train, horrible as it was. I wanted it to keep going, away from the white flags with red rising suns, away from the uniformed soldiers hungrily leering at us. But the train inexorably ground to a stop, brakes squealing. As Father helped us off the coach, I could see soldiers grabbing passengers' bags and suitcases, ripping them open and strewing the contents on the platform. Laughing excitedly, they snatched up watches, rings, pens, flashlights.

"O God," I breathed, "please protect us." I clung to Mother's dress as she moved protectively in front of me.

The closest soldiers studied us for a moment, grimaced, then turned to other passengers. Evidently they dismissed us as not worth plundering. I was so grateful for our guide's wisdom.

But we could not escape the mounting horror on the platform. As we turned to hurry away from the station, blood-curdling shrieks split the air, and I looked around. The soldiers were dragging the younger women out of the crowd. One girl clutched frantically at what appeared to be her husband. A soldier viciously kicked her in the stomach, her head flew back and he pushed her to her knees. Drawing his bayonet, he raised it like a machete and swung it down on her neck. There was the thump of a melon being cut in two. Her head rolled down the ties, and her bloodsoaked body sank onto the gravel roadhead.

Her husband, crazed with shock, leaped wild-eyed at the soldier who was turning to another woman. He reached out to throttle his wife's slayer, but the soldier wheeled, thrust his bayonet through the man's throat, and the husband collapsed onto his wife's corpse.

I stared transfixed. Father clutched my shoulder and spun me around.

"Walk!" he ordered. *"Walk* and don't look back."

We stumbled along, heads down, trying to blend in with the others fleeing. Night had darkened the city, and I flinched as shadowy forms rushed toward us. But in the orange light from burning buildings I could see they were refugees like us. On we hurried, I between Mother and Father holding their hands. From time to time I stumbled over corpses; whether they were children, men, or women I could not tell, only that all exuded the same sickening stench of death, with which I was fast becoming familiar. As we passed a strange-looking building on top of a hill, I could not help but crane my neck to peer at it. For the "hill" was really hundreds of stone steps leading to the building.

Father noticed my glance and said: "Sun Yatsen, his memorial." I stared back over my shoulder, fascinated. We had learned about him in school. Sun Yatsen was the "George Washington" of China who had helped unite it from a fragmented country ruled by warlords. In 1911 he became the first president of the new Republic of China. As my parents hurried me along I sadly wondered if my country would ever be whole again.

The dark buildings became smaller and farther apart, and I remembered that Father had said we were to rendezvous with our refugee group outside of Nanking.

As dawn lightened the east, we stopped at a hovel where a pig rooted in the mud. Father stepped up to the wooden door and knocked, using a special sequence our guide had directed. The door slowly squeaked open, a man squinted at us for a moment, then waved us in.

I could not see anything in the smoky darkness at first, only smelled the overpowering odor of humanity. As my eyes grew accustomed to the dark, I could see men, women, and children huddled on the floor, a small bundle next to each.

These were the people with whom we'd travel; twenty-seven of us would make the long journey to Chungking. Moving by night was safest. We waited until dusk fell, then stepped out into a starlit early winter night. My breath steamed in the frigid air, and I was thankful for my quilted clothes, dirty as they were. An unearthly squalling filled the air, and from behind the hovel came Father and other men dragging ancient wooden carts behind them.

"Haven't you any oil or fat to quiet this squeaking?" asked Father of the farmer who owned the house. "The enemy will hear us a mile away."

The old man laughed. "Oil you want? Find some and I will give you gold." He turned away muttering.

Father helped Mother and me into the cart with our bundles. Then he got between the long wooden arms like a rickshaw man and began pulling.

Our long journey had begun.

We bumped along through the night, past endless rice paddies, reflecting the starlight and barley fields blanketed by pale mist. *To travel fifteen hundred miles like this?* I wondered. I still wished we could have simply taken a *fanchuan*— a sailing junk—upstream to Chungking which, like Shanghai, was also on the Yangtze River. But Father shook his head. "It would not be safe, Neng Yee. We would be too obvious. We must go by land and travel by night."

By sunrise, our group lodged in a small hovel-like "hotel" in a rural village. I had difficulty sleeping. Finally, when I dozed off, I had a nightmare: Grandmother chased me with a big knife, then a buddha leaped down from its shrine and gained on me; when an enemy soldier grabbed me I awoke screaming. Mother comforted me, while others I had disturbed glared and muttered.

The next night trouble loomed. Our column halted. What was wrong? Father went up to find out and returned shaking his head.

"Just as I feared," he sighed. "One of the carts broke down; the rotten spokes gave way." He looked at our wheels and shrugged. "And we paid good money for these decrepit things."

A week passed as our five refugee families, along with some single people, pushed on. The little food we carried with us was soon gone. We begged and bartered for rice, bread, and pork from farmers along the way. Much of it was filled with vermin or spoiled. Often the bread would be black with dirt and we had to pick insects out of the rice. Sometimes we had nothing but boiled cabbage leaves for supper. Even the old duck's neck skin Grandmother forced on me would now have been welcome.

The winter air was bitter, and as Father leaned into the cart traces I could often hear him coughing. Then I would leap down to walk beside him. He wouldn't let me help but when the road was fairly smooth and pulling took little effort, he enjoyed talking to me.

One night when we could see the distant Yangtze glinting in the moonlight, Father jerked his head toward it. "The city of Wuhan is over there. A year before you were born, a terrible flood filled its streets. Many thousands of peo-

ple died; the city was under water for three months. But Wuhan thrives today."

I knew Father was trying to tell me that no matter
how bad things seemed, they would get better. But I could
not see how anything would be better after losing our home in
Shanghai. I even missed Grandmother's house. Most of all I
missed my Shirley Temple doll; I hoped my cousin was taking
good care of her.

Then Father's dire prediction about our cart came
true. One night while dozing I was rudely awakened by a
heavy jolt and clatter and found myself clutching the sides of
the tilted cart. A wheel had collapsed.

From then on we three walked, bags on our backs. For
the first several nights I looked on it as a lark. But after a week
my feet were blistered and my legs cramped with excruciating
pain.

"Father," I groaned one evening as we started on our
way, "why can't we stay in this little village and rest a while?"
He smiled gently and put his hand on my shoulder. "First, my
child, all of us in this group made a pact we'd stick together."
Then he said: "Neng Yee, this is our Long March. We must
not give up."

I thrilled at the words "Long March." Every child had
heard of this famous eight thousand-mile trek led by the
Communist leader, Mao Tse-tung. To escape rival enemy
troops, he and one hundred thousand loyal soldiers fought
their way across rugged mountains, rushing rivers, vast plains,
and swamps. After a whole year of constant marching, they
finally reached the city of Yen An in 1935, with only twenty
thousand soldiers left.

Though I didn't understand the politics involved, the
event had become an inspiring story to all children. And so
thinking of those courageous men I marched along with Father and Mother with a lighter step. Even talking about the
Long March must have brought good fortune. A commotion

arose at the head of our party; everyone was laughing and clapping. We rushed up to see one of our men holding a duck high.

"He wanted to join the group," he laughed, "and I welcomed him!" There was only a little piece for each of us, but oh, how I enjoyed feasting on that succulent roasted morsel. It made me homesick for the duck we used to enjoy in restaurants in Shanghai. Glazed with malt-sugar liquor, the ducks would be roasted over an aromatic fire of pungent fruitwood until a dark crispy brown.

Other poultry occasionally wandered across our path. But nothing could replace our worn shoes. After four weeks of walking, mine had become so frayed they flopped off my feet. I walked barefoot for a few days but my soles began blistering and bleeding. Mother pulled an old shirt out of her bundle and wrapped it around my feet, which helped.

Even worse than walking were the awful places in which we slept. Some were culverts, others copses of trees; the worst were the sheds we shared with livestock. "Mother, will we *ever* get clean?" I cried.

She tried to comfort me. "Neng Yee, there are things worse than dirt." Again, I did not realize how prophetic her words would be.

The air became colder and the land more rugged. Father said we were nearing the Wu Shan or Witch Mountains. I stumbled and fell on the stony path, cutting my hands on sharp rocks.

Crying, I stamped my foot and pointed toward the Yangtze far below us. "I don't care if the soldiers do see us, Father; we'd be better off *there*."

Wiping the blood from my hands, he said: "Then we all would die, my little one. The river there is full of bones of men and ships. It rushes like a dragon through steep gorges where there are *xuanwos* (giant whirlpools), *jiliu* (dangerous rapids) and *shuipao* (water spouts) which capsize even river steamers." He bandaged my hand, adding: "Still want to take the Yangtze?"

I smiled and shook my head. Father always seemed to make things right. I found myself wondering. *If my father on earth cared so much for me, how much more would my Father in Heaven love me?*

As the trail became even steeper, I found myself panting hard as we climbed higher and higher. Father said we were approaching the Sichuan Province. An older man began singing in a high voice:

> Eheu! How dangerous how high!
> It would be easier to climb to heaven
> Than walk the Sichuan Road . . .

I found myself entranced as he continued.

"His singing, Father," I said. "It almost sounds like poetry."

"It *is* poetry," he smiled. "The old man is singing a song by Li Bai, a great poet of the eighth century who wrote it for travelers like us."

I felt better. If a great poet could write of this terrible trail, then I could walk it, knowing he was celebrating wayfarers like me.

But it turned out we weren't the only ones on it. Five weeks on our journey and only ten miles from Free China, we stopped early one morning, bone-weary, at a deserted shed. Its two rooms were dank and dark, but after throwing quilts on the floor, we huddled gratefully and fell asleep.

A splintering crash jolted me awake. Had Japanese soldiers found us? A yellow light filled the room and, rubbing my eyes, I saw ugly-looking men carrying lamps standing among us. One kicked a traveler who was sitting up.

"Give us your money," he growled.

Father whispered, "Guerrilla bandits."

My heart froze. After all our struggle, would it end here?

I breathed a silent prayer of protection.

When they came to us, father handed over our last few pieces of jewelry. Others did the same. The guerrilla leader collected the loot, glanced at it, and spat on the floor. "Refugees . . . not even worth killing."

The other three held their lanterns close to the women, leering.

One pulled a frightened girl to her feet, then disgustedly pushed her back to the floor.

"She smells like a pig," he snarled. "They all stink." The leader waved at his companions and they strode out the door.

The room was silent except for the quiet sobbing of some of the relieved women. A young man jumped to his feet. "The vile snakes," he blurted, "let us teach them a lesson!"

An older man laughed: "Relax, don't try to show off your bravery. Thank Buddha we are alive."

I smiled to myself. Buddha? I *knew* Who saved us, the One Who had us sleep in filth so we smelled so awful. More and more I was realizing God's wisdom.

Then another man said, "We must leave now! They'll tell the enemy we are here to claim a reward for finding people escaping to Free China."

Quickly gathering what was left of our pitiful bundles, we fled the shed and hurried up the trail. Only ten miles to go! I held that wonderful thought in front of me like a carrot before a donkey. But soon even that didn't work, and I could only put one painful foot in front of the other.

Three hours later our guide held up his hand. We stopped, and word passed down the line: The border!

There was the clearing before us; the border was somewhere on the other side. But it was the clearing that struck fear in our hearts. About a mile wide, it had been opened by the Japanese to better spot escapees trying to make their way into Free China.

Couldn't we just run across it? I wondered.

Our guide pointed. In the distance a squad of soldiers, rifles ready, made their way toward us. We sank back into the trees. After thirty-seven days of living hell—walking, starving, suffering—was our journey to end here?

There was a chance, said our guide. "In this mountainous terrain, the Japanese do not expect much infiltration. Thus their guard is not as stringent at night. There is a chance . . . a chance."

It was about an hour until nightfall, so everyone started making preparations for the crossing. Since everyone expected to be killed, this involved washing faces, hands, and feet, and putting on the last clean clothing from their bags. All wanted their bodies to be clean so their god would accept them. Some were Buddhists, some Taoists, others followed Confucius. But to all, the ceremonial washing was important, even to my Mother who, though a nominal Christian, made sure Father and I washed, too.

Our party had only a small bucket of water, and when it came to my turn I felt I was applying more soil than I was removing.

Then, many in our group took out pens and began writing letters to relatives, instructing them what to do with the belongings they left behind in their former homes. *How did they expect their letters to be delivered?* I wondered. I thought of the advice of the ancient Lao Tzu who wrote: "Let the people regard death seriously and not move far from their homes. . . ."

Certainly, we all regarded death seriously, but none of us had followed his advice about leaving our homes.

But there was one thing *I* could do. As the sun sank behind the dark mountains I prayed: "Oh living God, can You hear me? I hope so, because right now we need the help of a

God Who is real. Please help us cross the border so the Japanese soldiers do not see us. In Jesus' Name, I pray. Amen."

Soon it was completely dark; even the stars were covered by clouds. Our guide whispered, "Now!"

Holding hands, Mother, Father, and I, along with the others, started walking toward the clearing. We were careful with our feet not to break even a twig. As we reached the stony open ground, we crawled on our hands and knees, only our heavy breathing breaking the silence. I kept waiting for the dreaded "Halt!" of an enemy soldier or the crack of a rifle. Then as we neared what we felt was Free China, we could not resist. All of us sprang to our feet and began running.

Even with the clearing far behind us we continued running as we did not know exactly where Free China soil started. But now we laughed as we ran. Finally, out of breath, panting heavily, we stopped and sank to our knees.

"Freedom!" One man shouted. "Freedom!" We all cried out at the top of our lungs. And then, with tears running down our cheeks, we raised our faces to heaven and sang our national anthem.

As we sang, I thought of the miracle that the Japanese border guards did not see or hear us. Could God have heard my prayer? Did He blind their eyes, stop their ears?

When we began walking again, I asked Father, "Where is Chungking? Shouldn't we see it by now?"

He patted my shoulder. "No, my child," he said, "we have many miles to go. It will take every bit of strength we have left."

I saw what he meant as our trail climbed higher into the snow-covered mountains. Though we now traveled by day, walking was more difficult than ever. Powerful mountain winds lashed us as we trudged on, heads down, squeezing our eyes against the stinging sleet blowing from snow fields.

Sometimes I found myself looking up at the soaring peaks sparkling in the cold winter sun and gasped at the stern beauty. At night, when we stopped in a small mountain village, Mother would rub and blow on my frostbitten hands and feet trying to bring them back to life.

Days passed as we stumbled down into a less frigid region and, when we came to a peaceful valley, some in our group wanted to stay there until spring. "We are so tired," sighed one mother, "we cannot travel anymore."

"But who knows when the enemy will come to *this* valley," pointed out an older man.

Since we had made a commitment to abide by the majority, we put the question to a vote.

"Go on," was the decision, and, dragging ourselves to our feet, we limped forward. Later that day someone up ahead gave a shout. We rushed up to see him pointing at a truck that evidently had been left behind by the Japanese. It was a strange-looking vehicle with a large upright cylinder at the rear. One of the men nodded. "Charcoal," he grunted, "I have driven this kind of thing. Gas from burning charcoal runs the engine. We must gather wood."

Enthused by the thought of riding, we scurried around hunting fuel. Men made a makeshift oven, putting dirt on top of the burning wood to covert it into charcoal. We also discovered some charcoal in the bottom of the trunk. Soon, all twenty-seven of us pilgrims chug-chugged toward Chungking.

Some of the group began to sing as we bumped along, but soon the words froze in their throats. Our ribbon of a road now clung to the side of the mountain, and it had narrowed drastically. Everyone was quiet as we inched along. I peered over the side of the truck and gasped. Just beyond our wheels the side of the mountain dropped straight down. I could see nothing but gray mist. As it cleared, I could make out rusted brown wrecks of trucks and buses that had plunged to the rocks hundreds of feet below.

"Everybody out!" called the driver.

The road had narrowed to where part of the tires hung

over the edge. While the brave driver inched the trunk past this spot, we walked behind it. I prayed for him.

Soon we were back in the truck again, and as the road improved so did our spirits. I could see a new brightness in Father's eyes. He looked at me and tousled my hair.

"Neng Yee, soon we'll be at Grandfather's house."

I looked around at the people who had made the trip with us. All of us had arrived safely. And all now seemed like close family; I would miss them, I knew.

Then down in the valley ahead of us I could see the lights of Chungking glimmering in the mist. "You'll find it foggy, my child," said Father, "and much different from Shanghai. But it is a beautiful city. I think you will like it. Most of all, we will be safe."

I smiled, watching the approaching lights. *Safe.* How pleasant that word sounded. No more worries about enemy soldiers. Enough food to eat. How good it would be to walk unafraid again.

We did not know that the enemy would soon reach us in a way none of us could anticipate.

6

WINGED DEATH

"There it is," said Father pointing upward.

I looked up the long flight of grey stone steps. At the top of them on a high hill Grandfather's house faded into the mist. As I looked at the old rambling building, which seemed to grow out of the earth, I suspected Grandfather would be just as unusual.

Ever since we had bid our fellow refugees heartfelt good-byes on our arrival in Chungking, I had an onslaught of new experiences and sights.

Chungking was an unusual experience in itself. A metropolis of hills at the conflux of the Yangtze and Jialing rivers, it was a stair-step city with thousands of stone terraces cascading down to the rivers.

Father had told me it was an important shipping and trading center for food grown in the nearby Red Basin, so named for its rust-colored sandstone, giving the earth its hue.

"Everything grows well here because of the constant moisture in the air and summer heat," said Father. "And that's why we can look forward to having enough to eat. For centuries, farmers have grown rice, wheat, sugar cane, and even cotton in the fields. On the high terraces, they harvest barley, sweet potatoes, peas, and grow mulberry and citrus trees, even tea plants."

After our meager diet on the trail my mouth fairly watered.

"But it is a very old city," Father continued, "more primitive than what you have been used to, my child. Even the dialect is different; you'll find the people more rural."

As we walked toward Grandfather's neighborhood I could see what Father meant. The stone and brick houses seemed so much older and poorer than our home in Shanghai.

I couldn't help but be entranced by the little outdoor businesses as we walked on past them. And I stared at a sidewalk dentist bent over a man who stoically leaned back against a tile wall. The dentist triumphantly extracted a tooth from his patient's gaping mouth, and I gasped.

Oops! I had bumped into an older woman carrying a basket of yams. Collecting them from the street, she shot me an angry glance and snapped: "Donkey!"

My face flamed with embarrassment; I turned to Father, and he patted my shoulder. "Don't be bothered, my little one. Chungking people are known to have tempers like their fiery food. There is an old proverb about these Sichuans: *First to rebel, last to yield.*

"Perhaps," he laughed, "that's why the Japanese haven't been able to take over their land!

"But also," he added with a lower note, "I have noted we 'foreigners' are not too welcome here." He glanced around. "With refugees streaming into the city from everywhere, I can see where local folk may well resent us. Thus, little one, we must be extra polite and show them we will be good neighbors."

With this in mind I tried not to stare. But I couldn't help but gape at the people I saw wearing white cloth bands around their foreheads. "Are they in mourning, Father?"

"I really don't know," he said, "but when we're settled at Grandfather's house, you can ask him. I'm sure he'll know."

When we reached Grandfather's house I stared in awe; five long flights of stone steps led up to the house perched alone on its hill.

"Be careful," warned Mother, "the fog here makes steps slippery." The climb seemed almost as bad as the Sichuan Trail. Huffing and puffing, we finally reached the top. It was noon when we knocked on the door. A pleasant-looking woman opened it, and when my father introduced us, her face broke into a smile.

Father turned to us. "This is Weng Shan, wife of my half-brother."

"And these," she smiled at the three children clustered shyly behind her, "are my children."

I was happy to see one of them was a girl about my own age. Weng Shan explained that my grandfather was at his bank and would be home later.

We were ushered into the kitchen for some hot food. It had been so long since I had anything tasty I had to restrain myself from appearing greedy. I also discovered to my astonishment what father meant by the fiery Sichuan food. Then we were shown the room in which we'd stay until we found a place of our own. About five in the afternoon, Father called me into the living room.

"Neng Yee, this is your grandfather."

I couldn't talk at first, just stood and stared. I had heard so much about him all my life and now here he was, a most interesting elderly gentleman. He smiled down at me, his little piercing eyes twinkling with humor. I couldn't help staring at his long pendulous ears—they hung down almost the length of his head. A cord trailed from one of them to a hearing aid tucked in his suit pocket. His gray suit seemed quite shiny, frayed, and lumpy as if he were wearing several layers of heavy underclothing.

Leaning on an elaborate carved cane, he was looking me over, too. Then he asked brusquely: "Child, don't you have any decent clothes to wear?" His gruff exterior didn't bother me, for under it I sensed a jolly, kind man.

"As you can see," said Father respectfully, "we had to travel as beggars and leave our clothing behind."

Grandfather turned to the granddaughter who was about my age and size and asked if she didn't have something I could wear. She smiled, bowed, and ran to her room. Mother got a dress from her sister-in-law, and Father put on one of Grandfather's old suits. That night at dinner the three of us once again looked like the Sungs of Shanghai.

For the first time since we left our home I felt among familiar surroundings. It was easy to see Grandfather's family was wealthy and cultured. Fine lacquered furniture, silk wall hangings, and beautiful antique vases graced the rooms. And Grandfather, himself, was a most gracious host.

At dinner he raised his tea cup. "In praise of tea," he said in his gentle voice, "let me quote the words of one of our eighth-century writers: 'If one is aching of the brain, smarting of the eyes, troubled in the four limbs or afflicted in the hundred joints, he may take tea. It's liquor is like the sweetest dew of Heaven.'"

He smiled at me. "Did you know, Neng Yee, the finest tea in China is grown right here in Sichuan?"

I felt encouraged to ask him about the white headbands I saw men wearing earlier in the day.

He laughed. "Let me tell you. Thousands of years ago a certain scholar recommended that men wear such bands to ward off headaches. And without questioning, or thinking about it, they continue to do so today."

He looked at me closely. "Now, tell me, my child, what does that teach you?"

I was too bashful to reply at first, but then answered: "Just because someone tells you something is so, doesn't make it right."

Grandfather smiled and turned to my parents. "A perceptive child, and one with good judgment." Turning back to me he said, "Yes, my granddaughter, never forget that. Don't believe everything you're told. Always think for yourself."

He laughed and turned to the rest of the family at table. "After all, I didn't get to be bank chairman by letting others think for me."

I was to remember Grandfather's advice in later years at a time when there was no laughter at all. And, in a sense, it would save my soul.

Life in Chungking was the beginning of much learning for me.

And another Neng Yee was to come forth. For as beautifully furnished as Grandfather's house was, it had no running water nor electricity, which was common for most homes in Chungking.

Some of our water came from an outside well, and I soon learned to be very conservative, using every drop threefold—for cooking, then washing, and finally cleaning. One of my duties was to fetch water from the Yangtze, carrying it in double buckets hanging from a shoulder yoke. The caramel-colored river was always thick with mud. We sprinkled alum into it, which caused the mud to precipitate, sinking to the bottom so we could dip relatively clear water from the top. As I drank it I tried not to think of all the ships lining the Yangtze docks, the people I saw washing their clothes and bathing in the river. But I never became ill from the water. As I approached my twelfth birthday, the daily trips up all those stone steps were excellent exercise, and I became stronger than ever.

Instead of the pampered child in Shanghai, I was learning to appreciate work. Instead of being catered to, I was learning to help others. Soon after our arrival, Father began working as a physician for the Bank of China employees. He now owned only a few shirts; since Chungking summers were especially hot and muggy, he carried an extra shirt with him to change into at noon.

He worked so hard I decided I could do my part by washing his shirts. I scrubbed them on a washboard and hung them out to dry. Ironing them was something else.

Sssst! I learned the skill of using a charcoal-heated flat iron. To test its heat, I wet the end of my forefinger with my tongue, then touched the hot iron. It had to steam with just the right hiss before I started ironing. And that heat required just the right amount of glowing charcoal. Too much, and the iron would scorch; too little, and I'd rub all day. I was proud when I learned to finish a shirt perfectly. Father gave me a strange look when I handed him his first bundle of clean shirts. But the thrill I got out of doing something nice for someone else was exhilarating.

I was also becoming less apprehensive, no longer the little girl who used to edge fearfully past the grinning Buddhas in Grandmother's old house.

One evening as I walked home from school it was raining as usual. The deep mud clung to my feet, and I had to trudge. Thank goodness, Grandfather had given me a flashlight, for it got dark early this time of year.

"There are some wild dogs that roam the fields, Neng Yee," he warned. "If any come near, shine the light into their eyes. Bad things seem to fear the light."

I gripped the flashlight as I walked, carefully studying the field. Suddenly, a dark low form slunk toward me. I became frightened and wanted to run. But something told me that would be the wrong thing to do. Whispering a quick prayer, I turned on the flashlight and pointed at the form. Two yellow eyes gleamed in the dark.

"Go away!" I shouted with a fierceness that surprised

me. The eyes disappeared. I felt stronger than ever. A resolute voice, I learned, can be most effective.

But a strong voice had no effect on Chungking's most prevalent bane: bugs!

One night I dreamed I was being stuck by a thousand needles. In the morning I awoke to find tiny red welts all over my body. Mother took one look and clapped her hands in horror. "Bed bugs!" she gasped. We took the bed clothes and boiled them. When I told my cousin, she nodded as if it was an everyday thing. "And it's not just them," she said, "it's also the fleas. They are everywhere."

I had wondered what the tiny black jumping things were that kept me busy scratching. "But it wasn't like this in Shanghai!" I protested.

"Neng Yee," she laughed, "you are not in Shanghai. You are in Chungking. And when you live in Chungking, you live with bedbugs and fleas."

One morning while I pulled the bed sheets from a bubbling caldron, Mother rushed up to me, her face filled with joy.

"Neng Yee, Neng Yee," she exclaimed, "we have our own home!"

I turned to her in disbelief.

"Yes," she said, "Father found us a house not too far from here. It's difficult finding places in Chungking with all the refugees, but I think you'll like it."

I was overjoyed, until I saw the dwelling.

Father seemed so proud when he brought us to our new home. But I could only stare in astonishment. The structure was a typical commoner's house. On the second floor, four families lived in separate sections. On the ground floor was a coffin factory and a place where pigs were kept. The coffins didn't bother me. To the Chinese, death is a familiar neighbor. But the pigs . . . *ugh!*

But Father looked so pleased; I knew he went to a lot of effort to find the place.

"Oh, Father," I exclaimed, hugging him, "it's wonderful!"

The nicest thing was that, around the same time we moved, my parents were able to enroll me in a boarding school run by American missionaries. The school was wonderful. Even though I had difficulty with the Chungking dialect, I enjoyed singing the rousing hymns and thanking God before every meal. The evening devotional services helped me realize how faithful God was in helping my family escape the war. And I felt sad when I thought of friends who were left behind.

I would often pray for them, and our country so torn by war for so many years. I even found myself praying for Grandmother and my cousins back in Shanghai.

My favorite place for prayer was a little park I found in my wanderings. It overlooked the Yangtze, and I would often sit watching the hills glow in the setting sun. Here I asked God to send me a friend, a real companion. My cousins were good company and kind. But I ached for someone with whom I could share my innermost thoughts. I had never had such a friend.

One day God answered.

While I was standing on our school grounds watching children play, a girl who was a senior came up to me. She said, "Wo jiao [my name is] Feng Yung Tat. Ni hao? [How are you?]"

"My name is Neng Yee," I answered. I liked this tall girl immediately; there was something special about her.

"I would like to be your friend if you want me to," she said.

I was thrilled, and we soon became close companions. Feng Yung Tat's father, Feng Yuk Cheung, was a famous

Chinese army general. Her whole family was devoutly Christian.

Though she was a few years older than I, we spent hours together. Not only did we enjoy girl talk, but Yung Tat would tell me a wonderful story about Jesus every day. We would pray together for everything from good school grades to protection for our families. One afternoon our prayers for protection took on special meaning.

As we stood on the school grounds an eerie wail of sirens rose over the hills. Yung Tat's face paled, and she grabbed my arm.

"Run, Neng Yee! Run! Enemy bombing planes are coming!"

We both began running toward an air-raid shelter. It was a large cave in a mountain of which there were many in Chungking. People crowded into it, and Yung Tat and I stayed close together. The place was dark and hot inside.

"Stay close to the entrance," whispered Yung Tat. She jerked her head toward the rear. "The air is awful back there."

A tremendous explosion split the air outside the cave. The ground heaved and people screamed. Distant explosions followed and the drone of planes faded. Then the siren began wailing spasmodically.

"It's all clear," said Yung Tat. "We can go out now."

We stepped out blinking in the blinding sunlight. Two blocks away a black pyre of smoke climbed into the sky, evidently the bomb strike that had sounded so close. Strangely, after the "all clear" everyone went about their business as if nothing unusual had happened. The herb seller went back to her stall, the man roasting ducks stirred up his fire, the street sweeper picked up his broom and swept up the pile of debris he had abandoned when the warning sounded.

Enemy bombing had become a way of life in Chungking.

But not to us newcomers. Father returned home late

one day after a particularly heavy bombing raid. His face was ashen, and his chopsticks tremored as he ate supper. Even the fatted pork mother prepared for him didn't seem to excite him.

"It was awful," he finally said. "I thought I had seen human suffering as a doctor, but not like this. I was on my way to a patient when the siren sounded. I rushed to a cave shelter, and it was so full of people that I found myself being forced farther and farther to the rear. I worried about being suffocated, since I have heard that such deaths have occurred."

He was quiet for a moment, then continued. "It wasn't suffocation that was dangerous this time. It was the cave's mouth. A bomb struck right outside and those who were standing near the entrance . . ."

His voice trailed off. Finally he said, "There was nothing I could do for them as a doctor."

The following day I saw something even more horrible. After school, Yung Tat began pulling me down a street.

"Where are we going?"

"Come," was all she would say. We hurried until we came to a mountain where many men feverishly dug with picks and shovels. It looked as if a landslide had taken place.

"It was a cave filled with people," whispered Fung Tat. "Yesterday a bomb buried the entrance. The people are still inside."

I turned away, thinking of all the poor souls walled into a tomb. The newspapers reported the next day that workers were able to save some of the victims, though most died of suffocation.

More and more, the air-raid siren became a regular part of our lives. Then one day I suffered my own trauma. Because the cave was so crowded, I had to stand near the entrance. A small group of men, women, and children raced toward us. Suddenly, with a brilliant flash and roar, a bomb exploded in the street. I ducked as clods of earth rained on me. When I looked up, most of those who had been running toward us were fragments. Some were still alive, but these were just bloodied bundles crying out in pain.

After these experiences I found myself dashing toward a shelter at the first sound of the siren. But there was a time I thought I'd go mad in one cave. Mother and I were at the market haggling with a vendor over onions when the siren sounded. We hurried to a cave, and Mother settled down, her back to the wall, and sighed: "Well, this will give us a chance to rest."

Our "rest" lasted two and a half days. The Japanese, evidently frustrated at not being able to bomb Chungking into submission, decided to go all out. Fleets of bombers flew over the city day and night for almost three days. While the city shuddered constantly from the bomb explosions, Mother and I huddled in that cave without food, water, or sanitation. The summer heat was at its highest, and the stench became so bad that the worst odors on our long march from Nanking seemed fragrant in comparison. And for the first time I found myself comforting Mother, rather than her soothing me.

Fortunately, so far our family, including everyone at Grandfather's home, escaped harm. Even his house, in its exposed hilltop location, was spared. But I worried more each day, praying that God would watch over us.

Then one August day in 1945, my prayers were answered. I was standing at the top of our stairs over the coffin factory when I noticed a commotion among a group of women gathered at the bus stop across the street. They worked in a nearby textile factory, and now they were exclaiming among themselves.

I ran down the stairs to them. "What is it?" I asked.

They turned toward me with the exhilaration people seem to have when they have important news to tell. "Don't you know?" exclaimed one.

I shook my head.

"Japan surrendered! The war is over!"

I could hardly believe it. The Japanese had long been such a formidable presence in China I could not visualize them surrendering to anyone. I always thought they would fight until the last man, with no Japanese left to surrender.

I couldn't wait for Father to come home. "Yes," he exclaimed, beaming, showing me his newspaper. "I heard it on the radio this afternoon at four o'clock!" He read the details to me about how atom bombs destroyed the big cities of Hiroshima and Nagasaki. Such weapons were incomprehensible to me. But it was clear to me now; our agony as an occupied country was over. Thousands of Chinese people now looked forward to returning to their homes and loved ones after eight long years of separation.

My mind reeled, and I stepped outside to try to collect my thoughts. For over half my life, my country had been under enemy domination. Now what would happen? As I mused, a distant popping sounded; I flinched thinking it was gunfire. Then I realized it was firecrackers. The crackling grew until all of Chungking seemed to be one gigantic string of firecrackers exploding in a mounting crescendo. Then down the street flowed a twisting dragon propelled by the centipede-like feet of the joyful men inside. I smiled at the celebration. The dragon, considered the most powerful and feared creature in folklore, would frighten away any evil spirits who would dare intrude on the happy celebration.

My own happiness soared when Father said that soon we would be heading home to Shanghai.

Later that week while Mother happily packed, and Father attended to details in finishing his medical practice with the bank, I slipped away to my little park on the mountainside overlooking the Yangtze. I sat on the grass, hugging my knees, thinking about the past and wondering what would come in the future. Warm summer sunlight flooded ravines and valleys undulating down to the river. Up from it floated the hoarse toot of steamboats, the low mutter of diesel tugs, and the distant chime of a bell of a junk under quilted sails.

As I mused at the shimmering river, I thought how much I had changed in the past four years since leaving my home in Shanghai. The pampered child who thought only of her doll and herself was no more. I had seen so much of life and death, of cruelty and compassion. And I had grown so much through learning the joy of work and responsibility, the blessing of friendship, and the binding love of family. I also had gained an inner toughness and self-reliance.

As I gazed down the long river disappearing into the mist, I felt that I was being prepared for something. What this task was, I didn't know.

God in His wisdom does not allow us to know what the future will bring.

If He did, I would not have been able to face it.

7

RED SUN RISING

Chungking's hills and rivers fell below me as the airliner lifted into the sky and headed east. I leaned into the window full of excitement. Mother and Father, who remained behind to finish up some last minute details, had sent me on to Shanghai. They had enrolled me in the Mary Farnham School there run by Presbyterian missionaries and wanted me to be on time for the fall session.

The last several days had been full of anxiety. Because of the multitudes of refugees returning to their homes, there had been no seats available on any flights from Chungking for months. Then with the opening of communications, Father found out where his brother, a captain in the United States Army, was stationed. Father had called him, and soon I was booked on a military plane bound for Nanking.

The plane was very spartan and uncomfortable, but I was so thrilled to be heading home to Shanghai I thanked God for my good fortune.

Far below I could make out Grandfather's stone house on its hilltop; my eyes misted as I relived saying good-bye to him. He had held me close for a long moment, his hand resting on top of my head.

"I give you my blessing, child. You have become very dear to me and I do not want to see you leave. But I know your future lies east in Shanghai, and so you must go."

Then he tousled my hair, and his little eyes twinkled. "And remember, Neng Yee, what you learned about those men in their silly white headbands."

I looked up at him and laughed. "I know, Grandfather, don't believe everything you are told."

Then we parted. He stood at the top of the long flight of stone steps as I slowly walked down them, looking back over my shoulder. He was wearing the ancient silk robe he usually wore at home and looked like an elderly emperor. He raised his hand in farewell. Then fog from the river swirled up, and he was lost in the mist.

"I will never forget you, Grandfather," I whispered as the plane droned on.

As we followed the Yangtze, now a silver ribbon curling through the mountains below, I remembered the legend Grandfather told me about the beautiful peaks that rise at the river's great gorges. "They are said to be goddesses who came down from heaven and fell so much in love with the earth they refused to leave it."

I smiled to myself. Beautiful as these mountains may be, I was so glad to fly across them rather than walk. I shuddered remembering our hunger, suffering the cold and the pain, and looking forward to enjoying a normal life again. *What would the future hold?* I wondered.

Back in Chungking I had asked Father if we could go to one of the fortune tellers who toss sticks and predict your future from the patterns in which they fall.

He thought for a moment, then said, "One of the lessons in my Catholic upbringing was that the Bible forbids us to go to fortune tellers or soothsayers. And a big reason for this, I feel, is that our little human minds are not geared to take all that information at once. I think it's like our electric-light system back home in Shanghai. Just enough electricity comes through the wires to keep the light burning at the right intensity. But what if a month's supply of electricity came surging through the line at once?"

"The light would burn out," I ventured, "even explode?"

"Yes, Neng Yee, and God sees to it that we know only what we need to know for the present.

"Besides," he smiled, "when you play kick bag and five stones with other children, would those games be as much fun if you knew how they were going to come out?"

I shook my head.

"Well, life wouldn't be as much fun, either, if we knew exactly what was going to happen everyday."

As it turned out, I am so very glad I didn't know what was ahead of me in Shanghai.

Before I realized it our plane was landing in Nanking, where I would catch a train for home.

When I told the man driving the pedicab I wanted to go to the railroad station, my heart caught. Suddenly all the evil and horror I remembered happening there flared in my memory, and I found myself clutching the sides of the pedicab.

The driver turned around and looked at me.

"You all right, Missy?"

I sighed, coming back to reality. "Yes, thank you," I replied. "The last time I was at the railroad station was in 1943, and it was not a nice place," I explained. "You can go on."

He continued looking at me, then said sadly. "Yes, I know what you mean. I was here all through that time. I lost my wife and children. But," he shrugged, "what can one do, but go on."

He turned to pedal, and I found myself grieving for all those who had suffered so much under enemy domination. *Yet,* I thought, *here was a man who had lost everything and was continuing on.*

I felt a surge of intense pride in my country. With people like him and all the others—farmers, fishermen, weavers, business people, yes, even us women doing our part—China would once again be a proud and progressive nation.

As the pedicab wheels hissed on the street, I thought of all the wonderful things my country had given the world. I remembered the night in Chungking at table when Father and Grandfather had begun enumerating all of the inventions we Chinese had come up with besides gunpowder, which everyone seemed to know about, such as the mechanical clock, cast iron and steel, the crossbow, the umbrella, porcelain, movable type, first printed book, first suspension bridge, rudders for ships, paper and paper money, wallpaper, and even the parachute with which a man jumped from a tower in Canton back in 1192.

I tired of trying to remember all of our inventions and it was just as well for the pedicab man was telling me: "We here, Missy, we here."

The train ride to Shanghai was far different from my last trip on this line. With the coach full of happy people and food vendors proffering their wares from every station platform, I found myself forgetting past memories.

Even Shanghai's railroad station now seemed a friendly place, especially with my mother's sister there to meet me. As we taxied to her apartment, we passed my grandmother's house. The stucco building looked deserted, and a chill went through me as I remembered those awful, lonely nights in the old dark wing.

A week later I was enrolled in the Mary Farnham Boarding School. The school had a pleasant campus. We girls lived on one side with our own classrooms and dormitories, and the boys lived on the other. There was no visiting back and forth without special permission.

Not long after I started, I knew I was in trouble. The school had high academic standards; I had difficulty keeping up. Soon I would face rigorous examinations that would decide whether or not I could go on to high school.

I prayed each morning to understand my studies better. But somehow I didn't feel I was getting through to God. What really impressed me was hearing other girls pray in chapel. The room was open around the clock, and often we'd go in there to talk about Jesus, read the Bible, and pray.

One day in chapel when I was a fourteen-year-old freshman, a friend, to whom I had confessed my worries about the exams, started praying for me. I was surprised; I had never heard anyone pray like that before. She seemed to be talking to Jesus as if He were standing right in the middle of us. I believed in God, yes, but He seemed so distant and far away.

"Oh Jesus," she said, "You know how much Neng Yee wants to pass the examination and how difficult she is finding her studies. Please, Father, in the name of Jesus, give her the wisdom and insight she needs."

When she finished, I thanked her, adding in awe, "You talk with Him like He is right here."

"*He is*, Neng Yee," she said softly, "He is. He hears us and I know He will help you."

"I would love to know Him like that," I sighed.

However, I still did not achieve that closeness with Him I had so long sought.

Then came the dreaded examination. It was scheduled for the coming Friday, and my classmates planned to spend every spare minute studying for it.

"Do you have a flashlight, Neng Yee?" a friend asked the day before the exam.

"No," I replied. "Why?"

"Tonight is our last night, and it's the only way to get

your studying in." We read under our blankets after "lights out."

I decided to call Mother and ask her to bring a flashlight to me.

But that afternoon something strange happened.

As I passed our school bulletin board I happened to see an announcement that an American evangelist would be speaking on the boys' campus Thursday night. Girls, it noted, would be permitted to attend.

Something nudged me to attend, but I immediately dispelled the thought. Listen to some preacher instead of studying for the most important exam of the year? How silly!

Still the thought persisted. Again, I put it out of my mind. Common sense told me study was more important.

Late that afternoon I had occasion to pass the bulletin board again. The little notice seemed to beckon to me. I was a bit irritated. But now I realized I was facing a decision. It was a choice between the elusiveness of God and the cold-minded practicality of the world.

I decided to go to the meeting.

The matron was surprised when I asked for a pass to attend when all the other girls were studying. And I forgot about asking for a flashlight.

That evening as I crossed the street to the boys' campus a fall wind rattling the dry leaves in the trees seemed to hiss: *Ridiculous . . . ridiculous . . . ridiculous.*

But as I neared the auditorium I heard beautiful singing, "Take My Life and Let It Be" and I completely forgot the exam. Soon I sat on the edge of my seat listening to the evangelist.

He spoke about God hungering for fellowship with us so much that He sent His only Son to earth so we could know Him better. And through His Son, Jesus, we could live life more fully and abundantly. "And even though His Son was rejected, tortured and killed, He still forgave us and stood ready to accept us," continued the preacher.

"All we have to do is admit we can't save ourselves," he stressed. "We must abandon ourselves to Jesus. Let Him take over our cares and worries.

"Trouble with us," he continued, "is we think we're so good we try to handle it all by ourselves. That's when we get into trouble."

As the evangelist talked I could see that was exactly what I had been doing. Oh, I prayed, but when it came right down to it, I was still the one in charge.

Suddenly, I realized how weak I was. Impulsive, impatient, so often a leaf in the wind, I realized how much I needed God.

When the evangelist invited everyone who wanted to accept Jesus as their personal Savior to come forward, I knew what I must do. With tears scalding my cheeks I knelt at the altar. The preacher kneeling with me, put his arm around my shoulder.

"What do you want, my child?"

Sobbing, I asked, "Do you . . . do you think Jesus would want me?"

"Oh, my child," he sighed, voice choking. "This is why I crossed the sea, to come here to tell you that Jesus is yours, that you belong to Him."

Then admitting to God that I was a sinner who couldn't handle life alone, I asked Him into my heart. I abandoned myself to God.

After the meeting I floated back to my campus feeling true acceptance for the first time. The sad circumstances of my birth, the rejection of my grandmother, didn't matter anymore. I knew I belonged to God, the Creator of all that is.

Singing, laughing, and crying all at once, I was approaching my dormitory when I saw a white beam of light stabbing the darkness. It was our school janitor making the rounds with his flashlight.

I found myself asking, "May I borrow your flashlight for tonight so I can study for my exams?"

He evidently was finishing his last round, for he handed it over and smiled. "Yes, you may use it."

As I walked into my dorm it struck me: When you obey God, as I did by going to that meeting, everything else falls into place, like finding a flashlight just when I needed it.

The next day I passed all my examinations so I could enter the next year of high school.

A few weeks later I was baptized. I did not know that soon this would be a very dangerous thing to do.

In the meantime my joy in the feeling of being *accepted* continued. Then another miracle occurred, which I believe was from God.

I came home from school for a weekend visit to find a cute two-year-old boy smiling at me from Mother's arms.

Mother chucked him under the chin. "Little Neng Yao, this is your cousin, Neng Yee." His little brown shoe-button eyes sparkled, and he gurgled.

"Oh, Mother," I cried, "he's so cute." I reached out and picked him up, and he nestled his little head against mine.

Little Neng Yao was the baby of my father's brother, a dentist, who was the U.S. Army captain who had helped me find air passage from Chungking. He had been stationed in Shanghai, and when he was transferred to Peking, little Neng Yao had the measles and was too ill to travel in the cold weather. So his parents left him with Mother and Father for the time being. Neng Yao had since recovered well.

Growing up alone, I had always wanted a baby brother or sister, and I had fallen in love with the tyke.

Then the miracle happened.

After Neng Yao's parents moved to Peking, my aunt

gave birth to a second son. Weeks turned into months and still the little two-year-old stayed on with my family. I had so much fun buying him clothes, dressing him up, even taking him to school to show him off to my classmates.

One weekend I came home to find my mother sobbing in happiness. She showed me a special delivery letter from my aunt.

You may keep Neng Yao and make him your very own son, she wrote. *We have enough children without him.*

There were no legal papers necessary. Neng Yao was a gift of love from his family to ours. This is common in China when one brother has more than one son and another has none. The son is joyfully welcomed by his happy new father. For it is a custom in China when a father dies that a son carries the head of the coffin and the daughter carries the foot. This signifies a complete family, and now we were whole.

Father and Mother were so taken up with little Neng Yao that weekend he became ours that I had difficulty finding out from Father about new developments in our country's government. We often discussed it at the dinner table. It seemed two powers were fighting for control of our country, and I was fascinated by what was going on.

I knew that since 1928 our country had been headed by the national government of the Republic of China under Chiang Kai-Shek. But now since the war was over he was being challenged by Communist forces under their leader, Mao Tse-tung. I knew Chiang and Mao had once fought together against the warlords who had fragmented China for centuries. But the two men differed greatly in their philosophies of government. Mao, son of a farmer, believed that instead of landlords and wealthy merchants owning the land, it should be held in common by the people. Chiang looked to the prosperous landowners and businessmen for support. And the two leaders ended up in violent opposition, their armies fighting each other for years. It was in 1934 that Mao and his Red Army led the famous Long March to consolidate their forces at the city of Yana in north central China. Now with World War II over, Mao had launched an offensive against Chiang to claim China for the Communists.

I wasn't quite sure which leader was best for us. Chiang Kai-Shek seemed to offer status quo and stability, while Mao Tse-tung promised new hope and progress for our country, which for so long had suffered under domination of warlords and foreign imperialists.

In my youthful idealism I found myself leaning more toward the leader Mao Tse-tung. Perhaps it was the romantic legend of his Long March and his philosophical quotations that impressed me. It was said that it was while standing on top of the holy mountain of Yen An and viewing the rosy sun rising like thunder over China he made his famous declaration: *"Tung Fang Hoong,"* which in English is "The East is Red."

When I finally had Father's attention over tea that weekend at home and told him of my feelings, he looked at me sadly and said, "Remember what Grandfather told you at the dinner table in Chungking when you asked about the men in white headbands?"

I nodded, sipped my tea, and lowered my eyes. "Yes, Father," I answered, "he said, 'Don't believe everything you are told.' "

But for an idealistic young person aflame with hope for her country, this was a very difficult thing to do.

8

THE ANGRY TIGER

Gunfire muttered in the night like distant thunder.

Father raised his head from his book. "They are coming closer," he observed quietly.

It was evening in Shanghai in late 1949. My parents and I were in the living room of the house they now owned. It was not the grand residence I knew as a child before Shanghai fell to the Japanese, which seemed a lifetime ago. But it was comfortable enough with a small garden in which mother grew herbs and a few vegetables. She was embroidering, and I was studying in preparation for entering law school at Soochow University early the following year. My little brother, Neng Yao, was fast asleep in his bed.

But none of us had our minds on our reading or work. For the Communist Army was advancing on Shanghai. The conflict had all started not long ago. I had been bicycling home when I heard my name being called.

"Neng Yee! Neng Yee!"

I braked and turned to see a friend rushing toward me, waving her hands.

"What is it, Chung Shin?"

She stopped to catch her breath.

"Did . . . did you hear?" she gasped. "President Chiang Kai-Shek and his government have left the mainland to set up new headquarters in Taipei, Taiwan!"

I stared at her for a minute trying to take it all in.

"Then Chairman Mao and the Communists will take over," I said.

"Oh yes; they are setting up our country's new capital in Peiping!"

Then it was settled, I thought. *All the years of fighting between the Nationalists and Communists were at an end.*

Not yet, we were to learn. Die-hard Nationalists and anti-Communists were battling Chairman Mao's army in many places.

I mounted my bike and pedaled home, the errand on which I had set out completely forgotten. As I rode up the busy Bund by the waterfront I wondered what would happen when the Communists took over completely. There were so many rumors. Some said all property would be confiscated. Others claimed girls would be forced to marry men not of their choice. During the past year many people left China, some for other countries, some for Taiwan, which was free of Communism.

Six months ago Mother had bid a sorrowful goodbye to our neighbors, the Lings. "So you are going to the United States?" said Mother.

"Yes," sighed Mrs. Ling, "our son is now running a prosperous restaurant in New York City, and he says we should come now when we can. He says we can help him in his business. We hate to leave, but. . . ."

"I know . . . I know," Mother consoled, taking her hand. "It may be the best thing."

I had asked Father what we should do and he held his hands out helplessly.

"Where would we go?" he asked. "None of our friends

or relatives in the United States or Hong Kong have offered to help us. We'll just have to stay and see what happens.

"After all," he shrugged, "it can't be as bad as some people say. But look, Neng Yee," he added, "your mother's sister has gone to Taipei, Taiwan with her husband and children. You enjoy her company. If you wish to join her, you have our approval."

It sounded inviting. For some reason I felt a bit queasy about the Communists. I couldn't put my finger on what bothered me. But there was something about them I didn't like.

Three days later found me on the windswept deck of a rusty freighter plunging in the grey waves of the China Sea bound for Taipei. After we docked, a pedicab dropped me off at my aunt's apartment. It was above an office, and when I climbed the creaking stairs and stepped inside her rooms I was shocked. There was no water or modern bathroom facilities. And since my aunt and her husband were starting life over, there was very little furniture. We slept huddled together on a quilt spread on a cold floor. It was winter and after a few such frigid nights I decided that life under the Communists couldn't be so bad after all. Besides, I missed my family, and when I returned home I had no plans of ever visiting Taiwan again, *ever*.

However, not long after I returned home, I wondered if I was right in returning. The streets of Shanghai were jammed with refugees streaming into the city. Men and women staggered under heavy bundles of household goods, or leaned between the handles of carts loaded with everything from babies and bedding to crates of wildly cackling chickens. Their faces bore the same fear that I saw in the refugees fleeing the Japanese when I was small.

One frightened woman dragging a little boy stopped to lean on a lamppost for a moment to catch her breath.

"Where are you from?" I asked.

She pointed to the west. "They killed my husband because he owned land," she said without emotion. "We have no place else to go."

She picked up her bundle and, pulling her boy behind her, was soon lost in the crowd of homeless people desperately seeking sanctuary in a city that was fast running out of hope.

Again Shanghai suffered as it had when Mother, Father and I fled an invading enemy some ten years previously.

Then in 1949 the Communist Army entered Shanghai.

That night in our living room my parents and I listened to the gunfire of advancing troops. The distant mutter of guns intensified to where we could hear the staccato of machine guns amid the blast of exploding shells.

Father rose and turned off the lamp. "The police station is nearby," he said. "There will be fighting there soon."

The gunfire rose in crescendo, and I found myself praying for my family's protection.

Suddenly there was a cannonade of explosions seemingly outside our front door, then eerie silence.

"It's over," whispered Father.

That night I couldn't sleep. *What will the world be like tomorrow?* I wondered.

It was a Communist world. A neighbor told us that on the previous night the local police had been marched out of their headquarters with their hands behind their heads.

"They have taken over the newspapers, radio station, airport. They are everywhere," she said.

Red Army soldiers *were* everywhere, but they seemed disciplined, not like the rapacious enemy troops of World War II. And we soon learned not to be afraid of them if we obeyed their orders.

As days and weeks passed, Shanghai was flooded with a torrent of "good news" about Communism. Leaflets were spread everywhere extolling the new order. Our newspapers and magazines painted bright pictures of how much better off our country would be.

Our old school books were whisked away to be replaced by new texts quoting Chairman Mao. "If you are a proletarian artist or writer," he stated, "you will extol not the bourgeoisie (upper class) but the proletariat and the working people."

I had to agree with that statement. My father was a hard-working person who gave of himself for the sake of his fellowman.

In our new history books we read how Mao prepared himself all of his life for his new calling. When he was a student in Peking in 1920 he read voraciously, listened, argued, and studied various governments. We learned how he was able to unleash the power of the common people for the good of China. "The force of the peasantry is like the raging winds and driving rains," he had written. "It is rapidly increasing in violence. No force can stand in its way." In paying tribute to peasants "with their rough, blackened hands" who would lead China's revolution, he asked, "Shall we stand in the vanguard and lead them, or stand behind and oppose them? . . . destiny will force us to pick an answer soon. . . ."

I thrilled at his words. For too long our country had been under the domination of foreign powers. Clearly he was the man for our time.

There were changes everywhere. When Chung Shin and I went to the movies we found that the American film we had anticipated seeing was gone. In its place was a Communist educational film. When we asked what happened to the other picture, the ticket seller fixed us with cold stern eyes, and snapped, "This is a better film."

Father came home one night shaking his head. "I went to the city health department today, and the man who had headed it for twenty-five years was gone. In his place was a stranger, Communist, of course." He picked up his chopsticks and began eating dinner. "From what I hear, it is like that everywhere; there is a complete changeover in government."

But if we thought Mao brought only changes in government and educational and cultural activities, we were shocked into reality on the 1950 Chinese New Year. It was the Year of the Tiger. In China, each year is named for a different animal, a practice that goes way back in time.

On New Year's Eve, firecrackers spit and sputtered in the streets. The usual serpentine dragon, which chased away evil spirits, writhed down our lane on the backs of happy, dancing men.

Fireworks exploded around my heels as I, with nine other girls, marched, holding billowing red flags and portraits of Chairman Mao. As we neared our house I saw my parents standing outside watching, and I proudly called out a signal for our formation. Waving our flags in unison and holding high Mao's portrait we chanted:

Brave Communists drove the Japanese army from our shores.
They stopped inflation and the endless corruption.
Beggars are no longer seen on our streets.
Our pride has been returned to us!
The great Chairman Mao will show us how to stand up to the world!

A few people applauded; then I broke formation and ran to my parents.

I bowed to them respectfully: "Your daughter gives you her love and best wishes for the New Year!"

Mother gave a sad smile, and turned her head toward the other girls marching up the street. "Is this how it is going to be with you?"

"What, Mama?"

"This marching business?"

"Oh, Mother. The Communists are Chinese. They have returned our country to us. We must show respect. Come, I have presents."

"Yes, and we must clean the house for the New Year."

Everywhere on our street, families were scrubbing, dusting, polishing their rooms and furniture for the New Year.

I carried out refuse from cleaning our kitchen. When outside I stopped and listened. The staccato of fireworks still sounded, and I sensed hope in the air. New Year always signifies hope to the Chinese, and everyone prepares for it with "off with the old and on with the new!" I stood for a moment in the cold midwinter stillness and thought. Soon I would be going to Soochow University Law School. Now under the new Communist regime, I expected a greater future.

"Neng Yee, don't forget we must wash our hair tonight."

"Yes, Mother, I'm coming."

Washing one's hair and putting on new clothes for the New Year were all part of the celebration.

"And I have your new robe for tomorrow laid out for you."

I thought about tomorrow. Chung Shin had asked me to go to the fortune teller with her tomorrow to find out what the New Year held for us.

"I don't think so, Chung Shin," I said. I remembered Father telling me the danger in this.

"Why?" asked Chung Shin, "is it because of what they've told you in that missionary school?"

"No," I retorted defensively, "I . . . I just don't think I should believe in some woman who tosses sticks."

"Oh, now you're too good for something we've been doing for years," she answered sarcastically. "Don't tell me," she continued angrily, "those Christian teachers have told you it's wrong." She tossed her head. "I know how they think."

She wheeled on me, fire in her eyes. "Don't let them fool you, Neng Yee. Chairman Mao does not believe in *any* religion. And look what *he* has accomplished. And don't count on that Christian business. It comes from the foreigners, doesn't it? And according to Mao they have brought all sorts of terrible things to China, including opium!"

I had never seen Chung Shin like this. She took a deep breath and added, "Didn't Karl Marx say that religion was the opiate of the people?"

"Oh, come off it, Chung Shin," I tried to laugh. "I'll go with you to the fortune teller tomorrow . . . for old time's sake."

After we parted, I thought. *What could be the harm?* It was just a diversion. It didn't mean anything anyway. I found myself becoming just a little irritated at letting those Christian teachers tell me what and what not to believe.

New Year's morning dawned bright, cold, and still, too still. But I was too busy at first getting ready for the day to notice it.

For this was the holiday when everyone would visit each other bringing New Year's greetings. Mother had already placed a large bowl of candy on the table for guests. And everyone was getting into their new clothes. Even little Neng Yao wore a new outfit. He was so cute.

But something was wrong. At first I couldn't put my finger on it. Then I realized. There was an unearthly stillness outside. No firecrackers. No happy voices. I glanced at Mother and Father. They hadn't seemed to notice. Instead, they were busy discussing which homes we'd visit. Finally, with everyone ready, we stepped outside.

Mother gave a little scream, her hand flew to her mouth. Father stood riveted, staring. I felt sick inside.

An ugly yellow sign plastered on our door screamed: DEPRAVED TIGER: YOU MUST CONFESS! Another on the gate declaimed: A RUNNING DOG SHOULD DIE. I couldn't believe it. The sound of a door closing quickly came from across the street, and I turned to see a frightened face at the window. A large banner flapped in the cold wind on the fence: TRAITOR TO OUR COUNTRY!

Mother broke into sobs, her shoulders shaking. Father put his arm around her and led her gently back into the house.

There was no New Year celebration in 1950, the year of the tiger.

Instead, it marked the beginning of a nightmare of terror. Aptly named, it was the year in which the Communists pounced on the city with full teeth and claw. Gunfire rattled in the streets. Later we heard there was rioting; people had been shot without cause and their bodies left lying where they fell.

"Revolution is no dinner party," Chairman Mao had said.

"A baby is born amid bloodshed," said Marx.

But when it came to my own family's blood, it hurt.

It happened after I had started law school at Soochow University.

I came home one evening to find Mother huddled in tears.

"Your Father has not come home," she cried, leaning into me. "Oh, my child," she choked. "What has become of him?

"I'll find out, Mother." Jumping on my bicycle, I pedaled to his office. There a weeping cleaning lady said: "Soldiers. They came . . . took him away."

I sped furiously to Communist headquarters. By now I knew that to get anywhere with these people, one must not act afraid.

"What have you done with my father?" I demanded.

"Oh, you must mean the so-called Doctor Sung."

"You know who I mean!" I pounded the desk.

"He has been arrested. That is all I can tell you."

"Where is he?" I demanded. "I must speak to him."

The official turned and walked away.

I went home so full of anger I didn't even consider praying for his safety. This was a time for action, I felt, not hopeful supplications.

Mother cried and Neng Yao kept asking, "Where, Daddy? Where, Daddy?"

Every day I haunted the local Communist headquarters demanding to see my father. Two weeks after his arrest I came home from school to find Mother waiting for me at the door, her eyes shining. "He is home. Your Father is *home.*"

I rushed into the living room to find him slumped into a chair, smiling at me. He was so thin, his face was gray and his eyes tired.

"Oh Father!" I rushed over and knelt at his lap. He placed a tremoring hand on my head.

"What happened?" I asked through tears.

He told how the Communist police came to his office and arrested him despite patients waiting to be treated. They rushed him to the top floor of the hospital where he was incarcerated.

"Day after day, night after night, they questioned me," He sighed.

"They were so ridiculous. They accused me of being a wealthy capitalist.

"They said my father owns the Bank of China. I laughed and said their party leaders should live as simply as my old father does."

His face pained. "They slapped me for that."

"They said I was a traitor for going to France as a young boy to study medicine.

"I replied that it was to bring real knowledge of medicine back to China instead of using ground bones and herbs. They hit me for that.

"They accused me of dealing with the 'foreign imperialists.' "

"How is that?" I asked.

"They said, 'You and your dog of a wife brought food and medicine to the missionaries in the Japanese prison camps. Your neighbors told us and we know it is true.' "

Father sighed. "So now it starts. Neighbor against neighbor. But I can understand. They went to our old neighbors and demanded they say something about me or they, too, would go to prison."

I put my arms around my dear father. "Don't worry," I said. "I am studying law. I won't let them do anything to you. Wait 'til I become a lawyer."

He waved his hand weakly. "We cannot think about the future, Neng Yee. We must face today. And the fact is our house . . . this house," he waved his hand around the room, "is being confiscated by the Chinese government."

"Why?"

Father coughed. "To repay the debt they say I owe the people of the Republic of China for stealing money from the hospital."

"Oh Father," I cried. "They can't make an accusation like that. It is a lie!"

He smiled gently at me. "No, my child. You must remember: whatever the Communists say is true, no matter how wrong it is."

Two days later our family was no different than what we had been the day we left Shanghai for Chungking. Only now it was four of us. Father had gotten an old two-wheeled wooden cart just like the one in which we started our trip to Chungking. In it we loaded all that it would hold. Then like a rickshaw man he got between the arms and with Neng Yao riding, Mother and me walking, hauled our few belongings to the new "home" assigned us by the Communists. No neighbor had the courage to say good-bye. Every door on our street remained closed with curtains down. Once again we were refugees.

With the wooden cart wheels bumping on the cobblestones, Father led us into a squalid factory slum district. Finally, he stopped before a decrepit building that leaned crazily toward the street.

"Well," I sighed, looking it over, "at least it has several rooms."

Father looked at me painfully and led us to our quarters. It turned out we would live in just one small room. I stared at Mother. She could only look at the ground.

The room was a shambles. Window panes were jagged splinters of glass, walls were crumbling and peeling. A stench pervaded the place; it obviously had not been cleaned for years.

"Where's the kitchen? The bathroom?" I asked.

Father gestured toward the building. "In there. We must share them with five other families."

The next day Father started work in a nearby factory as a doctor for the workers. That night he shuffled in the door late in the evening. As Mother served him supper she triumphantly placed something next to his rice.

"Fatted pork!" his eyes brightened. "Where did you find it?"

"Oh," she smiled, "that is a secret."

I knew Mother had walked miles and traded a piece of precious jewelry for this treat for Father. Seeing the love between them made me cry inside.

As he ate, Father said he had to diagnose and treat over a hundred patients that day. "It is tiring," he said, pushing his empty plate away. "But it is a job. And they pay me . . . some."

The pittance Father got for doing the work of five doctors was only enough to keep us with food. Mother made do with it the best she could.

At the university I threw myself into my studies. I vowed to become the best in my class, to be a high-ranking lawyer. Then *I* would have power. And with power I would take care of my family. Father again would be a respectable physician. And Mother would live in a nice house.

I could feel myself becoming hard. In this world I now knew no one would fight for us. I would have to do it all by myself. I would become smart and tough. I would beat the Communists at their own game.

9

WHERE ANGELS FEAR
TO TREAD

I'll never forget the first time I saw him.

It was lunch break on a balmy spring day at Soochow University. Two classmates and I exploded from the doorway onto a small square where we found a shady spot. We all wore the regulation blue Mao slacks and shirts that was now the "fashion" for everyone.

Laughing and giggling we opened our lunch packets.

"Did you have self-criticism this morning?" asked Chung Shin.

"Of course," I laughed, knowing my frivolity irked her.

"Did you stand up?" asked Ling Me.

"I couldn't think of anything really good," I grinned, "so I promised to never wear lipstick again."

"Were you *really* sincere?" Chung Shin grilled.

"I was this morning," I smiled.

"You should be more serious, Neng Yee," she scolded.

"A real glory is coming to China. We intellectuals must lead the way."

"Oh, Chung Shin," I laughed, "don't be so serious. Spring is in the air. Let's enjoy it. Besides," I rolled my eyes, "I was born in the Year of the Monkey. So I have a right to joke and have fun."

Ling Me, sensing tension, changed the subject. "I heard the Communists have actually stopped all business on Euzhow Road."

"Oh, the red-light district?" I said between mouthfuls of food. "What will happen to all the Singsong girls?"

"They will be re-educated, of course," said Chung Shin seriously.

I couldn't resist observing: "I don't think they excelled because of their intellectual ability!"

Ling Me and I broke into gales of laughter; even Chung Shin couldn't resist.

Suddenly, my breath caught. "Oh, boy! Look at that . . ."

My classmates turned to where I was looking.

The tall handsome man was striding across campus. What most impressed me beyond his fashionable western slacks and open Arrow shirt was his nonchalant walk. Self-confident appearing, he seemed oblivious to his surroundings.

"Western clothes!" I marveled.

"An upperclassman . . . Lam Cheng Shen," announced Ling Me.

The young man stopped at a secluded spot under a tree, sat down, and opened a book.

I was fascinated.

"Hong Kong money," noted Ling Me. "They say his family is very rich."

"Handsome, too," I sighed. "I'd forgotten men could look like that."

Ling Me snickered.

"He's years older than you," spat Chung Shin.

I smiled. "I always find older men more attractive."

"Forget it, Neng Yee," said Ling Me. "He's a strange one. A melancholy sort. A loner. He's never dated anyone at school."

"Hmmmm," I said, finishing my lunch. "Give me two weeks. I can change that."

Ling Me jumped to her feet and stared down at me. "You wouldn't *dare!*"

"Yes," I said, looking over at Cheng Shen. "Yes, a dinner date . . . give me two weeks."

"Trapped by your own words," muttered Chung Shin, "So bourgeois."

"If you lose, big mouth," cried Ling Me, "You have to do my homework papers for a month!"

"Mine too!" chorused Chung Shin.

As we walked back into the school building, I turned to look again at Cheng Shen under the tree buried in his book, and noted, "Don't worry, I'll get him to take me somewhere."

Later as I bicycled home, I savored the memory of the handsome young man.

However, something deep down within bothered me. If I had been close with the Lord, I would have known He was trying to tell me something about this young man. But I had long since rejected thoughts of Christianity. That was a phase of my girlhood, now over.

I was living in the real world now. A world of hard, cold facts in which I was learning to live by my wits. And quite well, too. For I was excelling in my studies. When I graduated, I would soon become a big potato who would make others jump.

Right now, however, I had to find my mother and bring her home.

"Aiiyaa! Where you go?" An old man under a yoke of

dressed ducks leaped out of my way, and I realized I had not been watching where I was bicycling. I apologized and searched down the narrow cobblestoned lane where I expected to find Mother. Soon I could hear the loud clicking of the ivory tiles of the mah-jongg game she loved so well.

I found her hunched over the tiles with several other women.

"Come, Mother," I said, "I'll take you home."

Reluctantly, she rose and climbed onto the back of my bicycle. As we wormed our way through the twisting alleys, I said, "You are not talking. How much did you lose?"

"My pillow stood straight up this morning," she snapped. "Always a good omen for me."

"You had money to gamble, Mother," I sighed. "Where did you get it?"

"It is not appropriate for you to question me," she said querulously. "But I will tell you anyway. It was an old silk scarf; I got a good price for it. Tell me, Neng Yee," she said, "where could I wear it these days?"

We pulled up in front of our "home" and went inside. As drab as its exterior was, it was now much different inside. I had scrubbed the walls and floor until they shone. Father had replaced the broken windows. And Mother, who could do quite a bit with very little, had made it "homey" with herb pots artfully decorating the windows and pictures cut out from magazines decorating the walls. She was going to put up a picture of Chairman Mao she found in the newspaper. "For political purposes," she said. But I put a stop to it. "I do not want Big Brother watching me."

That night at dinner I wasn't as talkative as usual. Mother, who always joked that I had been given acupuncture with phonograph needles, asked: "What is the matter, Neng Yee?"

"Nothing, Mother," I sighed, my mind on Cheng Shen again.

Father looked up. "I don't blame you, my child," he said. "It is the terrible conditions under which we live. We should have left China when the Japanese were defeated."

"Nonsense!" said Mother. "Who expected it to go this way?"

I put my chopsticks down with a sharp rap. "Look!" I snapped. "I will be a big potato for the Communists. You just watch. Okay? If the front door is locked, I'll go through the back!"

Mother looked down at the table sorrowfully. "Neng Yee," she sighed, "you were not raised to be a 'potato.' What a common expression."

I laughed. Even the next day I chuckled to myself as I bicycled downtown on Hangkow Road, remembering Mother's reaction. As I turned the corner the chuckle died in my throat as I saw a crowd of people in front of one of the city's big cathedrals. Acrid smoke filled the air, and I pedaled over to see what was going on.

Orange flames leaped from a bonfire on the church steps. A line of soldiers fed the flames with books passed hand to hand from inside the cathedral. A cluster of priests and nuns huddled outside the great carved wood doors. Blood ran down the faces of some of them, and their black robes were torn.

I turned my head and bicycled on, pushing the image from my mind. Soon I approached Guangzhou Road where I stopped for a red traffic light.

There he was, Cheng Shen, sauntering amid the surge of pedestrians crossing the street. He passed so close to me that I could have reached out and touched him. But with pounding heart I kept my hands firmly fastened on the handlebars.

That night I dreamed about Cheng Shen.

A few days later in the university assembly hall as my

friends and I watched a propaganda film on Chairman Mao's great plans for our country, I saw Cheng Shen sitting a few rows away from us. I nudged Chung Shin and Ling Me and pointed to his handsome profile.

When the film, with its blaring martial music, ended, I quickly led my friends to the entrance and waited. As soon as Cheng Shen emerged, I loudly announced to my friends: "Did you ever see Shirley Temple in 'The Little Colonel?' It's my favorite film forever!"

Ling Me's hand shot to her mouth in horror. Chung Shin glared at me. Soon we all were moving along with the crowd down the hall. We stopped in front of the university bulletin board.

"Neng Yee, that was stupid!" whispered Ling Me. "You must be more discreet."

"That was a serious film we watched," said Chung Shin, iron in her voice. "It is an offense to joke about our glorious history."

Trying to control my giggles, I said, "I *was* serious, Chung Shin, it's just that I prefer . . ." And I silently mouthed "Shirley Temple."

Before Chung Shin could retort, Ling Me spoke loudly, "Look! *His* name."

She was pointing at a notice on the bulletin board. It read: "Volunteers are requested on Saturday to clean up the university grounds. Please do your duty for the betterment of all. Those wishing to serve, report to Cheng Shen."

"Not on Saturday," wailed Ling Me. "Not me."

Chung Shin turned away quickly. "I have a paper due."

"Oh," I announced importantly, "It is *important* to volunteer. We must show the proper spirit!"

Chung Shin shot me a nasty look. Ling Me had already disappeared.

Saturday found me kneeling in a long line of girl volunteers laboriously clipping grass with hand shears. The noon sun burned my neck and sweat stung my eyes.

This was not what I had planned on.

In desperation, I got up, stretched my aching back, and then walked over to a work detail of men weeding a large flower bed. I found Cheng Shen on his knees carefully cultivating a small patch of flowers.

I cleared my throat, twice. Finally, he looked up.

"Do you need help here?" I asked, my throat suddenly tightening. "I have completed my assignment."

"Thank you, no," he said, turning back to his work. "I am nearly finished."

I frantically searched for something to say. Finally: "I have heard it said that our great Chairman Mao does not approve of flowers for the new China." Where did I get *that* idea from? I thought to myself.

"Perhaps he prefers weeds," Cheng Shen grunted.

"We had beautiful flower gardens when I was a child," I ventured lamely. *Why doesn't he respond?* I wondered.

He continued cultivating, silently digging with his trowel, not looking up. Finally, I dared not stand watching him any longer and reluctantly retreated to my fellow grass-clipping workers.

At the end of the day we lined up at a shed to return our tools. As I stood waiting, hot, tired, and dirty, I regretted wasting a Saturday. Suddenly, there was a movement at my side.

I glanced up to look into Cheng Shen's soft brown eyes. I caught my breath in surprise.

He offered me a yellow tulip.

"Cut it by mistake," he said quietly. "It seemed a waste to see it tossed out with the weeds." He gave a sad smile. "We have not been properly introduced. I apologize."

For once I couldn't speak. Then he was gone.

That evening I carefully pressed the flower in one of

my school books. Then, I held the book close to my breast, lost in rapture.

"What is it, Neng Yee?" It was Mother looking up from her embroidery.

"Homework, Mother."

Mother gave that little cough which signified she didn't believe me.

Before I went to sleep that night, I had devised a plan.

I had heard from a classmate that Cheng Shen was planning a trip to see his parents in Hong Kong. Everyone knew Hong Kong was a shopper's paradise. I also had volunteered to sell tickets for an upcoming concert to benefit poor children. I decided to put the two together.

The next afternoon I bicycled to the apartment building where Cheng Shen lived. It was in an affluent section of the city, and I felt a little apprehensive as I glided up in front of the tall building. Again came that whisper within: *Think, Neng Yee, think.* But I brushed it aside, dismounted, and walked up to the lobby. I stopped for a moment outside the glass door to check my reflection. Reaching behind, I pinned my blue Mao jacket back to make it more form fitting, fluffed my hair, took a deep breath, and walked inside.

Apartment 21 was up one flight and down the hall. I hesitated a moment before knocking. Again came that odd feeling of something not being right. But I had come too far to pay attention to it now. I knocked.

Cheng Shen opened the door. From behind him drifted the notes of "Some Enchanted Evening" playing on a phonograph. He looked surprised.

"Oh . . . uh, it's *you!*" I exclaimed, pretending to be flustered. "Do you live here? What a surprise. I've been going door to door selling concert tickets for a benefit," I continued rapidly, "for poor children."

I gazed up helplessly.

Cheng Shen scratched his head. "Oh, uh, concert

tickets?" He smiled. "I'm sorry, but I'm leaving for Hong Kong tomorrow."

"Oh, but the concert is two weeks away," I said. "You will be back in time." Suddenly feeling that I was giving myself away, I added quickly, "I mean surely you wouldn't miss two full weeks of classes?"

He looked embarrassed. "Your tickets . . . are they expensive?"

I looked at the floor a moment, pretending to think. The notes of "Some Enchanted Evening" had ended, and the phonograph needle was click-click-clicking at the end of the record.

"Oh," I said brightly, "I just thought of a wonderful idea. As you must know, nylon stockings have disappeared from Shanghai. If you would consider making a purchase for me in Hong Kong, I would be *most* grateful."

I thrust some money at him. "This should be enough. And," I added, smiling sweetly, "in return for your kindness, I will purchase two seats for the concert. The tickets will not cost you a fen."

Cheng Shen glanced quickly over his shoulder, looked down at the carpet, and up at me. "You are asking me to buy nylon stockings?"

"Oh," I demurred, widening my eyes, "but if it is too much of a problem for you . . ."

Cheng Shen smiled, and shook his head. "No, I'll be happy to buy them for you." Then, looking down at me as if he was seeing me for the first time, he ventured, "I . . . I suppose we should eat somewhere before the concert?"

"Oh! Dinner and a concert? It almost sounds like a 'date,' " I exclaimed, my eyes fluttering. "But, don't worry," I laughed, "I never eat much. It will not be expensive."

I turned and retreated down the corridor.

"Neng Yee!" he called, leaning out the door.

I stopped and looked back. He laughed. "Do you always carry so much money for shopping?"

I smiled brightly at him, clattered down the stairs, and pedaled home like the wind.

Mother was waiting for me outside our hovel, her face anxious. Little Neng Yao clung to her skirt.

"Your father is late coming from the factory clinic," she cried. "Something has happened."

"It takes him longer, Mama, now that he has no car to drive."

"It is not the bicycle," she said ominously. "There was a raven at the window this morning."

"Mama, you worry for nothing."

"Don't patronize me! I can read the signs. I'm going to see Shek Tong Ting now."

Shek Tong Ting was the local fortune teller. I followed Mother, taking Neng Yao with me. Mother turned into a doorway. The small cubicle was hazy with joss stick incense. A Buddha squatted on a wall shelf. Mother placed a picture of Father on the table before the wizened ancient woman who sat impassively regarding it. Sticks lay on the table.

"He was born before dawn on September 11, 1900," Mother said faintly.

The woman calculated something on her bony fingers, then swirled the sticks into the air; they clattered on the table. She studied them for a moment, then croaked: "A dark cloud hangs over him at this moment."

Mother groaned. Leaving Neng Yao with her, I raced outside to my bicycle, leapt onto it, and pedaled furiously toward the factory clinic.

Part of the way there a glow filled the night sky, and soon I saw soldiers torching a row of low buildings. As orange flames crackled from the flimsy wood structures, soldiers were herding hysterical Singsong girls into a truck, their painted faces grotesque in the flickering glare of the burning buildings.

"Ha!" shouted a soldier seeing me coming. "A Singsong girl all scrubbed clean!"

He ran toward me; I tried to dodge, but he grabbed my handle bars, sending me sprawling into the street.

Clambering to my feet, fire in my eyes, I grabbed my bicycle back and shouted at the soldier: "My father is Doctor Sung at Hwa Tung Textile Clinic. He is late coming home; I am on my way to find him."

"This one's mind is almost as quick as her body," he sneered.

Another soldier rushed up and grabbed me. "She is soft under her jacket. Like a young pigeon."

"Don't touch me!" I spat at him. *"Animal!"*

At this an officer strode up. "What is it?" he demanded.

"She was escaping, Comrade Lieutenant."

He studied me. "You don't look like a Singsong girl."

I explained my mission and showed him my identity card. "I am a law student at Soochow University."

The lieutenant studied my card and returned it to me with a small bow. "I am sorry; my men were overzealous, Sung Neng Yee."

"May I go now?"

"Of course. But it is not wise to travel alone at night. Shanghai still contains many dark elements. It will take time for our New Order to eradicate them all."

I mounted my bicycle to leave. "Thank you, Lieutenant," I said.

"Your card," he said, handing it back to me. Then he added, "The New Republic of China will need dedicated lawyers to interpret the new order."

"I intend to be at the top of my profession," I said, and rode off.

Lights burned in the factory clinic, and I walked into the entrance to find a clerk sitting at a desk reading a book about Chairman Mao.

"Excuse me," I said, "I am the daughter of Dr. Sung. Is he still on duty?"

The clerk did not look up from his book. "Sung? He is not known to me," he muttered.

"Not known to you?" I exclaimed. "Impossible! He has practiced here for some time."

I pushed past him into a corridor. The hall was jammed with lines of tired-looking men and women waiting in front of harried-looking doctors. But I didn't see my father.

Then, for some reason, I pushed open a door marked "Lavatory." On stepping in, I found my father on his knees, scrubbing the floor.

"Father!"

He looked up in surprise. "Neng Yee . . . you should not be here."

"Mama is crazy with worry."

He looked down at his brush. "Stay off the floor, please," he murmured. "It is still wet."

"What are they *doing* to you?" I cried.

"This is part of my re-education," he sighed, "I am under 'the submission of the people.' "

I turned and pushed my way out the door back into the crowded hallway.

"Dr. Sung is a clean man!" I shouted. "A patriot! He loves and serves his country. . . ."

A woman attendant rushed over, pushed me into a corner and not unkindly hissed, "Shut your mouth, child! You will only make it worse."

I rushed home to tell Mother and collapsed on my cot crying.

The next day in class as the professor lectured, I

couldn't erase the image in my mind of my poor father on his knees scrubbing a toilet for the "New Order."

"Neng Yee!"

I looked up. The professor was glaring at me. "You are not with us today," he said.

"I'm sorry," I said, "what you were saying reminded me how much Chairman Mao suffered for us."

He seemed satisfied, and continued. "As I was saying, over-population and modern technology are Capitalism's own seeds of self-destruction. Eventually in such deluded countries machines will replace people, and the masses will forget how to work. Their societies will collapse from within. That is why every citizen of China must experience labor training. The time is fast nearing when we will be a 'classless' nation. A nation of laborers for the common good."

As he talked, I envisioned my father's slender fingers trained to perform the most delicate surgery wielding an ugly scrub brush. I could not resist raising my hand.

"Yes, Neng Yee?"

"Excuse me, Comrade Professor. But why are we studying law if there will be no court hearings?"

A ripple of gasps from classmates filled the room.

The professor, obviously discomfited, cleared his throat. "The Party is deeply concerned with human rights," he stated, "but counter-revolutionary activity *must* be controlled." He glared at me. "What prompts such a question? You must be specific."

"Well, I agree the Party's policy of change is vital to China's future," I answered. "But what provision is being made to protect the rights of the innocent who have been or will be unjustly accused?"

His face flamed. Then addressing the whole class, he barked, "Chairman Mao has repeatedly told us, 'A revolution is not a dinner party!' " Then, turning to the class, he said,

"There will be no more such senseless questions. We will get back to the subject."

In the tense silence that hung in the air for a moment before he began lecturing again, I knew that I had stepped over an invisible line.

10

A MANY-
SPLENDORED THING

Stringed instruments played in the background, and a waiter hovered at our elbows. Cheng Shen and I smiled at each other across the white linen-covered table. The luxurious restaurant was most unusual for the ascetic People's Republic. But Cheng Shen seemed to have ways for knowing just the right place.

I gazed enraptured at my escort in his perfectly pressed pink sharkskin silk suit. His earlier coldness and withdrawn attitude had been simply shyness, I decided, a fear that someone might reject him. I certainly could relate to that, having been rejected myself so often as a child.

Moreover, in our talk this evening, Cheng Shen had told me how he had suffered from tuberculosis as a young boy and had not really enjoyed a normal childhood. I awakened from my reverie to find him watching me.

"A strange smile," he said softly.

"Because you came back from Hong Kong," I said, "I am pleased."

"I had to deliver your stockings."

"Yes, but your family is in Hong Kong."

He leaned back in his chair and smiled. "But the good memories are here, Neng Yee." He laughed, sat up, and picked up his chopsticks. "Anyway, I could never be comfortable as a British subject. 'God save the Queen' and all that."

"Please tell me about your parents," I asked, chin in hand, adoring him.

"Why?" He said uninterestedly.

"Because they are your family!" I replied in surprise.

"Oh, there is not much to tell. My mother has small feet. My father has numerous concubines." He shook his head. "I don't know how many half-brothers and sisters I have." He began eating.

"Is that all you can say?"

"Isn't that enough?"

"I think you have built high walls about your life."

He put down his chopsticks and smiled at me. "Are you a student of psychiatry now?"

I lowered my eyes and began eating my kung bao chicken.

Later that evening we sat in the concert hall, waiting for the program to begin. It was warm and stuffy, and I attentively fanned Cheng Shen with my program. I looked up to the balcony where I knew my two classmates, Chung Shin and Ling Me, would be perched. They were there, peering down at me. I raised my program in a gesture of triumph. Ling Me beamed; Chung Shin tossed her head.

The beautiful music rolled over us like an ocean wave, and I was swept along with it in the warm loveliness of being with the man I had now vowed to marry . . . whether he realized it or not.

Months passed, and before I realized it Cheng Shen and I had been going together for a year. He had since graduated from Soochow University and was working in a local court. From time to time the subject of marriage came up and Cheng Shen always demurred. The last time it arose, he answered moodily. "I don't know, Neng Yee," he sighed, "maybe it's because of all those years with tuberculosis. But you know, I never thought I would live very long. So I have never wanted to take on the responsibility of a wife and family."

"Oh, Cheng Shen," I laughed. "You are too morbid." And in truth he was. As Ling Me so often chided me, "What do you see in that moody man? And *you* being so opposite," she continued. "You're always cheerful, making jokes, ready to go every morning. But *him* . . . he always looks as if he has lost his last friend."

"That's just why he needs someone like me," I replied. "I would be his very best friend for life."

But it looked as if it would never happen. We continued seeing each other and in 1953, when I was ready to graduate from Soochow University, I pressed him again. We were walking along the Bund boulevard watching the teeming Yangtze river traffic.

"I make such a low salary at the court," he argued.

"But I will be graduating with honors," I countered. "They have already promised me a good job as an assistant professor teaching history and political science to government soldiers at Tung Tsi." I nudged him and added, "And I was the only girl chosen from my class for this assignment. Just think of what you'll be getting."

He didn't seemed moved, so I added, "Look, Cheng Shen, I don't care how much you'll make. It doesn't matter to me *how* we live . . . just so we live with each other."

He sadly shook his head, started to put his arm around me, then quickly withdrew it. That didn't bother me. For in China one does not demonstrate one's affection in public.

On my graduation day, Cheng Shen sat in the audience. When they called my name to come up for my diploma, I walked forward, glancing out of the corner of my eye at Cheng Shen and my parents, who sat in another row, beaming at me. I held my head high, for I was the third honor student from the top in a class of 375 graduates.

After the ceremonies I introduced Cheng Shen to my parents. My parents seemed pleased to meet him.

"My daughter tells us you were a great help with her studies," said Father.

Cheng Shen smiled embarrassedly. "I doubt that she needed my assistance."

Mother thought for a moment, then said, "You know, I may have met your mother—before the war—at the French Club."

"It is very possible," said Cheng Shen. "My mother found pleasure in gambling."

"If only we all could go there now to celebrate," she sighed.

Father laughed. "Why? You would like to have dinner with ghosts?"

"If only ghosts came they wouldn't charge us for the meal!"

We all broke up with laughter.

Later that day I brought Cheng Shen to our little "house" for a celebration dinner. As we bicycled through the mud-paved alleys amid the noisy bedlam of squatter families living in lean-tos, I glanced at Cheng Shen to see his reaction. But he didn't seem to mind.

"A long ride," I said. "I apologize for the neighborhood."

"It is of no consequence," he said. "I studied eleven years to be a puppet judge in the courts of the people. I have no illusions."

I was glad to hear him say that as we pulled up in front of our little "house." Mother was in the street drawing water from the common spigot. She looked up, and dashed into the house.

As we stepped in, Cheng Shen sniffed and sighed, "Could *that* be the aroma of roast duck?"

Mother smiled in pleasure.

"Mother has been cooking for days," I said, kissing her. "You know, for a woman who has had servants most of her life, nothing stops her."

Father, Cheng Shen, my little brother, Neng Yao, and I sat down at the table and began enjoying the appetizers. Mother busied herself with other hot dishes.

"Mother, sit down," I called over my shoulder.

"I can't. The omelet will burn."

I turned to Cheng Shen. "It's done with tomatoes, taro root, and boiling sugar."

He smiled and turned to Father. "Your daughter tells me that you have been assigned to a factory clinic."

"Yes," I interjected bitterly. "His hours are endless. One day he treated one hundred thirty patients! What kind of work is that for a gifted doctor?"

Father turned to me and patted my hand. "Neng Yee. You must learn to restrain your feelings."

"Yes," echoed Cheng Shen, "the walls have ears."

"Then let them hear the truth!" I exclaimed.

Mother set the steaming omelet on the table. "Oh that child," she sighed. "She has always been like that. Very quick to state her mind. We don't know how to change her."

Cheng Shen smiled. "I know." Then he laughed. "Are you certain she is Chinese?"

Laughter broke out. At its sound, I suddenly caught myself wondering what had happened. Then I realized, it was the first time since we had moved here that laughter had filled this little room.

A few months later it was a decidedly different mood in the classroom of the Tung Tsi "speed school" to which I had been assigned. Once it had been a famous architectural school; now it was more of a walled fort. And instead of students learning freedom of expression in designing living spaces, it was populated by young soldiers learning ways of thought control.

The young men seated before me that first day looked so malleable. I could tell some were sophisticated city boys. Others were from the country. The rural students looked like so many we met on the fields and mountains on our long trek to Chungking.

Some were my age, twenty-one, others were much younger. I felt very proud standing before them.

"My name is Sung Neng Yee," I began. "I have been given the opportunity of teaching you two courses—history and political science. You have been selected to study here because you are all brilliant soldiers." I stopped for a moment to let that thought sink in.

"Now our great government is giving you the opportunity to be brilliant scholars as well. This is a privilege of our great new Republic . . ."

I stopped for a moment, suddenly realizing I was sounding just like my professors at Soochow. Was I falling into the same trap?

No! I told myself. There were many benefits of cooperating with my government—prestige, esteem, pride, and the hope of a glorious future. Despite the terrible things that had happened to my family and to others I knew, it was all a part of the process, I reasoned. And I *would* be a part of the process. We were promised a beautiful dream. And I would sacrifice to see that dream come true!

I continued speaking. "Yes, you all have been given a great privilege. For this is an intensified course. You will gain six years of knowledge in three. If you study hard, sacrifice," I looked around the room at the faces attentively leaning into me; for the first time I felt the heady thrill of power, of moving minds and hearts toward a goal I had set. "Yes," I emphasized, "if you study hard, sacrifice yourselves for our common

good, you will become contributors to our country's great new
Republic." On closing, I threw my clenched fist in the air and
cried: "Long live Chairman Mao!"

At this the students jumped to their feet, lifting their
fists in the air, and shouted: "Long live Chairman Mao!"

I had them.

My weeks and months at teaching went well. Though
I chafed at the rigorous controls of being checked in and out
of the building and of having my classes strictly monitored, I
felt I was pleasing the authorities.

I told Cheng Shen this one afternoon as we bicycled,
our usual pastime in a city where entertainment was limited.
He was especially moody this afternoon. I had told him a
week ago that if he was not interested in our marrying, then
we should stop seeing each other. I had hoped it would
prompt him to come to his senses. Instead, it threw him into
an emotional tailspin.

A few days later my father came to me. "Neng Yee,
what have you done to Cheng Shen?"

"Why?"

"He came to me yesterday and said he was going to
kill himself if you stopped seeing him." He sighed. "Why
don't you two get married?"

I shook my head. "Father, it is too difficult to explain."

That afternoon as we bicycled down the Nanking East
Road, I tried to cheer him up. For a long while he wouldn't
say anything, just moodily stared ahead.

As we coasted down a street to the waterfront, we
came upon a large group of elderly men practicing *taijiquan*,
the rhythmic, slow-motion calisthenics done by people since
ancient times. The old men were standing on one leg and
slowly turning their torsos in the centuries-old ritual also
called "the boundless fist."

I called over to Cheng Shen. "Maybe when you and I
are old and gray, we too can come down here and keep fit. I

guess it will be the only physical thing we do together," I giggled.

It broke the ice, and for the first time that afternoon he laughed.

"Come on," I said, "let me show you where I used to live."

As we headed toward the area where I had lived as a little girl, we passed a church. It was now being used as a warehouse, its doors shuttered. However, it still had a cross on top. It seemed to stand out bravely against the sky, and my heart caught.

"Do you still believe in Jesus, Cheng Shen?" I called.

He glanced up questioningly. He said he had once been a Christian, just as I had been.

Before he could answer, I said, "I don't. There is no God. Who can believe such superstitions anymore?"

I pedaled on, the church and its cross falling behind me. I took Cheng Shen's silence as agreement. As we entered our old neighborhood I thought how much I had grown since my parents and I had been driven out of it at the point of guns.

First Grandmother's "prison" house, the long march to Chungking, the bombings there, law school, and now here I was, a respected teacher for the new People's Republic of China. I was so much wiser.

As we bicycled down my old avenue with its palatial homes in park-like grounds, I pointed out familiar landmarks along the way.

"My governess used to take me for very controlled walks along this street," I called to Cheng Shen.

"A 'controlled' walk?"

"Shirley and I were in the wagon. The governess was forced to pull."

"Shirley?" he asked quizzically.

I laughed. "She was an American movie star about my age."

He started to say something; then his voice froze.

A formation of soldiers in the green uniforms of the People's Liberation Army jogged up the street toward us. We pulled over to let them pass, and they clumped past.

Cheng Shen wiped his forehead. "For some reason I always think they're coming after me."

" 'Fraidy cat," I laughed, though after my experience at night with the soldiers raiding the Singsong house, I, too, had held my breath as they approached.

We rode on and stopped in front of the large home where I used to live. For a moment I couldn't talk, seeing myself playing on its lawn with my Shirley doll. Now a sleek limousine with a red flag on its front fender was waiting in the drive where my father's Mercedes used to stand.

"It was bombed during the war," I said softly, "but now it's restored. I'm glad they didn't change it. I understand a big general lives there now."

"The privileged elite," snorted Cheng Shen. "I'm sure he has orderlies to press his uniforms, wipe his shoes until they shine like mirrors, put toothpaste on his brush . . ."

"And rush up with a handkerchief when his nose runs!" I added, laughing.

"You always find a joke in everything. A rare trait," he said, remounting his bike.

"Laughter is more useful than tears," I replied.

"And more beguiling."

I gave Cheng Shen a long look. He had never been so warm and pleasant. I felt so thrilled, I called out: "We must finish this day with music!"

"Let's find a piano," he called back.

"A piano? Do you play?"

"Only when the moment is right . . . like now."

Cheng Shen said he knew of a deserted club that had

been closed by the Communists because they said it was decadent. "I believe there is still a piano there," he said.

Fifteen minutes later I followed him through the back door of a building. We walked through a dark hall and stepped out into a small ballroom. The windows were shuttered, but there was enough light to see a small piano on a little stage.

Cheng Shen stepped over to it, sat down, riffled through the keys, and began playing.

"Oooh," I thrilled, "Brahms' Lullaby."

Then abruptly he shifted into a boogie-woogie, his head thrown back. I couldn't help but jitterbug to it. He looked over his shoulder and laughed. "Wait until your Communist students see you now!"

"I don't care," I laughed. "I love it."

Finally, out of breath, I sank down on the bench next to him and laid my head on his shoulder. He resumed playing Brahms and when I put my arm around his waist he stopped and said softly. "I think we should be getting on home now."

It was night, and silvery moonlight flooded the old cobblestone streets. The two of us silently walked our bikes up to his building. At his door, we stopped and looked into each other's eyes.

"Do you always see friends to their door?" he asked.

"Special days should never end," I murmured.

Together we walked up the stairs and down the hall to his apartment.

His hand trembled as he unlocked the door. It was dark inside, and Cheng Shen did not turn on the light. Moonlight flooded the room from the large window looking out on Shanghai's skyline. Cheng Shen walked to the window and stood there looking out; he seemed to be wrestling with himself.

I leaned against the bedroom door frame, tremoring inside.

"Cheng Shen," I whispered.

He turned. I held out my arms. "We do not need words," I said huskily.

Two months later when Cheng Shen learned I was pregnant, he wanted to get married right away. For some reason, the promise of a child settled his conflicts about marriage, and he was as delighted as I.

My parents both gave a big sigh of relief and printed the traditional red invitations to announce the marriage to their friends. In the meantime, Cheng Shen and I joined the long line of couples in the big government building to get our marriage application papers. As we inched toward the harried-looking clerk at the window, we exchanged long glances.

"Please keep your head down," whispered Cheng Shen.

"Why?"

"You look too happy. It may be considered counter-revolutionary."

I giggled, squeezing his hand.

"I can think of a bit of legislation that is quite pertinent at this moment," he continued.

"Yes, your Honor," I answered in a dutiful tone.

"The progressive family law of 1950 eliminated the old practice of a 'bride price.' "

"Just sign the paper," I giggled, "and you get a bargain!"

As we filled out the long government forms at a tall table, Cheng Shen looked around and whispered. "What if they ask us about improper relations?"

I looked at the form and started to reply, "There's nothing like that . . ." when I realized he was joking. I gave him a stern look but could hardly control my giggling.

We had the traditional wedding portrait taken by a photographer before his painted backdrop. The photographer draped a length of white lace over my head and shoulders, and I was a bride.

On July 1, 1955, our wedding was celebrated with a supper in the restaurant of the Ging Jung Hotel. There were five big round tables of guests; my father made a speech wishing us long life and happiness, and everyone toasted us heartily.

We returned to my parents' "home" where we spent our wedding night in the little curtained-off bed corner. With the two of us almost swallowed by the quilts and comforters, Cheng Shen propped his chin on his hand and looked down at me.

"You know," he whispered, "kissing in the new China is not only in questionable taste, but quite possibly unhealthy. I read that in the paper this morning."

"Doesn't it depend on the parties involved?" I replied.

He leaned down and kissed me long and hard. Suddenly, he sat up and said, "Ouch! I just lay on a rock!"

"Not a rock, silly," I giggled. "An egg. Two dozen, I think."

He dug around in the covers and with an astonished look came up with several hard-boiled eggs, dyed red.

"An old custom," I whispered, "to bring us luck."

"Do they have to be *red?*"

"It is the color of fertility."

"They've already worked their magic," he smiled. Then, looking straight at me, he said, "Promise me something, Neng Yee."

"Anything, love . . ."

"Teach our son to laugh."

"Oh yes, my darling," I whispered. To myself I promised, *I will teach not only him but you to laugh, to enjoy life to the fullest.*

I did not know that in a few months my child and I would both be condemned to death.

11

THE CRUCIBLE

It was hot and humid that summer morning in 1955 when I faced my crucible. Ill with the distressing morning sickness of my first pregnancy, I had spent the night in the school dormitory as I did sometimes instead of taking the long, late trip home. Cheng Shen agreed that it would be easier on me.

Outside of awakening early and vomiting, I had no idea that this morning would be different from the rest. In the common bath area, I washed, dressed, then breakfasted quickly on some rice. I could not stomach anything else this morning. My drab blue jacket and slacks, loose and baggy as they were, could not hide the fact that I was decidedly pregnant.

My clothes were already sticky with perspiration as I walked toward the auditorium for our regular 7 A.M. staff meeting.

Sick physically, I also suffered emotionally from the increasing pressure on all the staff by the Communist regime. The bureaucracy seemed bent on making everyone a mindless segment of a huge political monolith without individuality, hope, or personal freedom.

Justice for the individual was dispensable. Why, I wondered, had I studied law when every day landlords were shot without trial and their property seized? Religious leaders were pulled from their beds in the middle of the night and never heard from again. Intellectuals were stripped of their positions and sent to hard labor camps to be "re-educated."

Through it all, Cheng Shen and I were enjoying fewer and fewer moments of relaxation together. A week ago we had spent a rare afternoon walking in the beautiful Yu Yuan Garden in Shanghai Beach. Built in the Ming Dynasty over four hundred years ago, the ancient garden with its beautiful walkways and bridges that appeared to float over the shimmering waters seemed to be the only peaceful place left on earth.

We stopped on a bridge where Cheng Shen clenched the stone rail and sighed, "What kind of world are we bringing our child into?" He looked down into the mirror-like waters. "My friend Geng Sho with whom I work cut his wrists yesterday. He couldn't stand the persecution."

He turned and looked at me. "We're all under persecution, Neng Yee. Without you I think I would have done the same as Geng Sho."

I clutched his arm. "I know, I know. It is as they say, 'The nail that sticks out gets hammered down.' Some of our professors have disappeared. No one knows, or will say, what happened. Every day I hear shots outside the school and see soldiers hurrying by. There is talk of a firing squad in a field near us where they daily dispense 'justice.' "

We stood quietly, staring into the tranquil waters, realizing that the bright promises we had embraced in our youthful idealism had as much substance as the mist which now hung over the garden towers around us.

With the persecution came the disheartening fact that no one could trust others anymore. Spies were everywhere. Even in our own school we were learning to be careful about those with whom we shared honest feelings.

Now, on this hot muggy morning, as I approached my school's auditorium door, I hesitated. For days someone on the staff had been singled out to be cruelly interrogated in the morning meeting by Communist officials while the rest of us sat mutely by. The answers would be written down, and the one under scrutiny would be required to press his or her thumb print on the paper. Some of these people would not be seen again. This was just one of the many harrassments we had been undergoing. "True, loyal members of the state have no fear of these truth sessions," stated a Party official. As he smiled at us, I could only think of a cobra I had seen in our zoo.

"Comrade Professor!"

I glanced up from my thoughts. The auditorium guard was holding the door open for me, and I stepped through.

About fifty pale-looking people sat in a circle of chairs facing each other. I was surprised to see Chung Shin, who held a university clerical position. Usually, only teaching staff attended these meetings. She shot me a quick look when I came in and turned away.

"You are late, Comrade," barked the Communist official in charge. "Not a good example to be setting for your students."

"I'm sorry," I replied, "I have not been feeling well."

"One's responsibility to the state takes precedence over personal feelings," he snapped, "something you have obviously yet to learn."

Suddenly it was clear.

I was the one to be interrogated today.

"Your family history is troubling to us," he said in an accusatory tone.

"How is that possible?"

"Your father, Dr. Sung, lived abroad—France for fourteen years," he began, reading from a file in his hand. "He completed his medical studies at the University of Lyon. Your mother was president of the YMCA and was known to have strong American sympathies."

"She helped where she could."

"Your grandfather was chairman of the Bank of China. We hear he has escaped to Brazil with his riches."

"And my mother's family were wealthy sea merchants for generations," I interjected. "They gave the great Hong Ying library to Shanghai. But," I took a deep breath, and shifted uncomfortably in my chair, "It is all in the past."

"Why did your family stay in Shanghai when your relatives fled with their personal fortunes?" he pressed.

"My father said we must stay!" I replied, wondering what he was driving at. "When the stock market collapsed and all money was converted to Japanese yen we became refugees. But still my father would not leave China!" Sweat was beading on my brow. "Please, may I have some water?"

The official ignored my plea. "At what age did your parents enroll you in the McTyier Christian School?"

"Nine or ten, I'm not certain."

"*Why* did they send you to a foreign missionary school?"

"I don't know . . . for the instruction, I guess."

"Isn't it logical to suggest that they did this because they had strong Christian sympathies?" He stepped back and folded his arms.

"They are not really religious. My father had some Catholic instruction in France . . ."

"But," he interrupted, his tone more menacing, "after the war you were enrolled in a boarding school—also Christian."

"Yes, the Mary Farnham School. It was Presbyterian —it was rated very high academically."

The officer leaned down to within inches of my face.

"Is *that* when you became a Christian?" he snarled.

I gasped in astonishment.

"Why . . . I haven't been a 'Christian' for years. I was young . . . impressionable. It was just something you did while in school . . ." My heart pounded. "Please, some water?"

The officer smiled sardonically. "Why do these questions make you uncomfortable?"

I shifted in my chair. "My baby resists sitting so long."

The officer turned to the others in the group.

"Did Assistant Professor Lam ever indicate to you she professed Christian beliefs?"

All of them solemnly shook their heads.

"Do any of you have pertinent evidence that could be presented at this first meeting?" he demanded of them.

First meeting? I fought to control myself. One thing I had vowed to do was not become fearful or upset. I had seen other professors weep and break down at these interrogations.

"First meeting, Colonel?" I pressed. "With respect, I do not understand. I have never done anything against the People's Government."

"This is a matter of your dossier," he growled. "It must be determined if you are a Christian."

"But I have already explained," I protested.

"All Christians *must* declare themselves," he retorted angrily. "It is a matter of census . . . as must the Buddhists and the Taoists. . . ."

Suddenly, Chung Shin, who had been sitting quietly in the circle, stood up. "She married a man from Hong Kong. He brought her nylon stockings. He smuggled them into China!"

I looked at her in disbelief. She plopped down, and looked at the floor.

The officer stared at me for a long minute.

"So . . ." he seemed to savor the plum given him. "So . . ." Then, with iron in his voice, he said, "Smuggling is a serious offense. This will take consideration. Now you must write about your life from the beginning. Reconsider every event including your time with the missionary school and the Presbyterians."

An orderly came up with writing paper, a pen and ink, and put it on an empty chair next to me.

"You must return all paper that is used . . . even the false starts," he said.

He motioned the rest of the assembly to leave. They departed hurriedly, some stumbling into chairs, obviously relieved to escape.

I looked up pleadingly. "But my family. My baby. He is due soon. I must go home."

The officer's face was stone. "Consider this a chapter in your autobiography. The more you write, the sooner this matter will be closed. I will leave now. But be sure you write truly and complete."

The room was empty, except for a guard sitting at the door. The only sound was a distant muted shout of soldiers counting cadence as they marched past the auditorium. Occasionally I could hear a distant sound of rifle fire.

I began writing my life's story, my pen seemed to scratch loudly as I inked the characters on the paper.

In China, the family name gives meaning to a person. I write this with true awareness that the history of my family is of deeper importance than who I have become . . . After the defeat of the Japanese in 1945 my father brought us back to our beloved Shanghai. I was thirteen years old . . .

As I continued writing, the memories of my days at Mary Farnham School flooded back on me.

I remembered the soaring stained-glass windows, the chapel that was open twenty-four hours a day. I found myself enjoying the thought of its quiet, restful sanctuary.

My pen hurriedly inked characters. *As self-criticism and confession are the first steps to social reform, I will attempt to explain my involvement with Christianity at this impression-*

able age. It began like a tiny seed planted in my spirit. I was away from my parents and lonely for something . . .

I stopped, the end of my pen pressed into my chin as I remembered being in the chapel singing "Take My Life and Let It Be," the girls holding lighted candles. I felt warmed by the memory, but the words I wrote were deliberately cold.

At a time of personal stress, I did profess to be a Christian. It was the night before we faced the Middle School entrance exam . . .

I thought of that wonderful night when the American evangelist spoke, of how the Presence of Jesus Christ seemed so real to me.

I continued writing: *The strong emphasis on high test scores made me apprehensive. I had to deal successfully with the examinations. To do so would bring pride to my parents and better opportunities would be mine for the future . . .*

I thrilled again when I remembered asking Jesus Christ into my heart and the strong feeling that He was present with me.

However I wrote: *But when I left the Mary Farnham School, it became a distant memory. By the time I reached sixteen years the Christian God was forgotten. That experience from my childhood has no bearing on my life today in the new China. I now look to our great Chairman Mao for instruction and guidance.*

I signed my name, put down the paper, and looked around. The guard was gone, but the door was locked. It was obvious I was incarcerated here until morning. As I lay on a rug trying to sleep, a strange tapping sounded at one of the high windows. I startled, but then realized it was only the sound of gnarled tree branches hitting the glass in the wind that was moaning outside.

I awakened feeling stiff and sore. The little one within me seemed to be protesting by the way he moved around.

Soon the Party official was back. He picked up my "confession" and read it.

"Your writing is too specific. As if you were hiding something."

"I am not a writer of fiction," I said. Then, feeling bold, I asked, "Colonel, may I ask why you are bothering with me . . . a 'little potato'?"

"Your father was educated in France. He may be a spy!"

I laughed. "A spy! He has absolutely no talent for it."

"You do not see yourself as part of the masses," he said accusingly.

"Colonel, I respectfully invite you to our 'home.' You will see how we live with the masses."

A ghost of a smile played around his lips. "So," he said, "you have been forced into a simpler life. Do you find it acceptable?"

My baby squirmed within me, and I looked at the floor. "I miss the laughter."

The colonel finished reading my paper.

"Yes, I see where you have been falsely indoctrinated. Religion will ultimately disappear from human history," he noted. "But it will be a slow process of re-education. Old ideologies and cultural habits from the past cannot be eliminated in one generation. The era of pure Communism is a prize for the future. That will be China's millennium! For now it must be determined if you are worthy to assist us in our goals."

I gazed up at him, unmoved. "Will it always be unfair like this?" I asked. "I cannot see past the injustice, the falsely accused, the innocent killed."

He became cold. "Perhaps you should write again in more detail!"

Tears ran down my cheeks. "Colonel, can't you see my

situation. I am about to give birth. My baby needs adequate rest."

The officer's face softened for a moment, then it froze again. "I will leave now," he said, "But I must warn you. Another man will come to take my place. You'll find him not as patient as I."

A guard escorted me to a lavatory where I drank thirstily from a spigot. I was taken back to a small room with a desk, the door locked behind me. I leaned against the desk trying to sleep. But I couldn't help again remembering that evening at Mary Farnham School when I accepted Christ as my Lord. Hot tears scalded my face and I whispered, "I talked to You when I was a young girl. Do You remember my name?"

I seemed to feel His presence and fell asleep.

A loud crash awakened me. I blinked awake to see a woman in civilian clothes flanked by two soldiers standing over me. She kicked the desk again viciously.

"Get up, slut," she snarled. "How can you sleep so late? An indulgence of the lazy capitalist class. The revolutionary masses have been at work for hours!"

"May I please request some water? Just a glass?"

She leaned down with the look of a tiger savoring a fallen doe. "You must learn self-discipline."

"But I have nothing further to confess."

She nodded at one of the soldiers who drew back and slapped my face.

The room turned black and I felt myself sagging to the floor.

"We will help you remember," she snarled. "Stand up!"

I was jerked to my feet.

"We demand a full confession of your counter-revolutionary activities," she screamed. "You will begin by admitting you are a Christian!"

I gathered strength to speak. "If it were true, what is the crime? Our constitution guarantees religious freedom for all the people."

"You play games!" she screamed.

A blinding flash filled my senses, and the floor came up at me. Recovering my vision I looked into the boot of the soldier who had struck me in the face. He was standing over me. I could not get up.

An arm pulled me up. I stood, swaying unsteadily.

"You accepted an honored teaching position wearing a mask of lies," shouted the interrogator. "Did you intend to infiltrate the minds of our brave soldiers with your decadent beliefs?"

I wiped blood from my mouth with the sleeve of my jacket and murmured: "That is absurd."

"Why did you marry a man from Hong Kong who is not a member of the Party?" she hammered.

"I . . . I came to love him," I choked.

The interrogator spat. "Love is a bourgeois conceit! It has no place in a classless society."

Drawing myself up, I looked at the interrogator in the eye and said icily, "You speak of a classless society, yet you deliberately separate those whose background was more privileged than your own."

She froze, her small eyes narrowed, and she lunged, slapping me with her full might.

Again, lightning filled my head. I staggered backwards across the room, trying to keep my balance. Even the two soldiers' faces were full of surprise.

"No background?" she screamed. "Explain yourself! Whore!"

My mouth full of the salty taste of blood, I said quietly: "It is your manner of speaking. The cutting way you express yourself. It is perhaps the custom in Northern China but not . . ."

She lunged at me again, and I flinched; but this time she did not strike me. Instead, she concentrated on what I suspected was her real intent.

She stepped back, pretended to inspect her fingernails, and in a quieter voice said: "You see? You betray yourself. We must all eat from the same rice bowl." Then advancing on me, her breath hot on my face, she demanded: "Now you will answer 'yes' or 'no.' Are you a Christian?"

This was my Rubicon. For an instant, the temptation was strong. *Why not deny it?* A dark voice seemed to whisper to me. *After all, you believe in your heart, and God certainly knows*, it wheedled. *Why not satisfy this brute with a simple "no" and save yourself further torture?*

I could feel the warm blood on my chin and thought of Jesus on the cross, blood running down His face.

"He may be distant from me," I gasped, "but I will not deny His presence."

My interrogator fairly pulsed with hate. Thrusting her livid face into mine, she demanded. "Answer me, whore! Yes or no?"

Now I could see my Savior clearly, looking down at me from the cross with love and understanding. I was glad for the blood running down my face, the pain in my body.

"Yes or no!" screamed my interrogator, spittle spraying me.

"Yes! Oh, yes!" I cried out joyfully, enthusiastically. "Yes, I *am* a Christian!"

At my declaration, the interrogator exploded in a demonic fury. Shaking with rage, she stepped forward to strike me again, then stopped, turned to the two soldiers with her and shouted, "Take her out and shoot her!"

Russell Wong and Julia Nickson-Soul star as the lovers Lam Cheng Shen and Sung Neng Yee in *China Cry*.

Colonel Cheng (Philip Tan—4th from left) and Chinese soldiers shout Communist slogans in a scene from *China Cry*.

Sung Neng Yee (Julia Nickson-Soul) arouses the suspicions of the state when she starts challenging the official party line.

Sung Neng Yee (played by Julia Nickson-Soul), pregnant with her third child, carries her son Chuin Man (played by Louis Tan) as they cross to freedom from Mainland China to Macao.

Sung Neng Yee (Julia Nickson-Soul) must serve out her husband's sentence at forced labor until he returns from a visit to his dying father in Hong Kong.

Philip Tan stars as Colonel Cheng, a ruthless, dedicated servant of the state, determined to break the independent spirit of two young lovers in the feature film *China Cry*.

Julia Nickson-Soul stars as Sung Neng Yee, who finds her independent spirit and love of life in deadly conflict with an oppressive and repressive state, in the feature film *China Cry*.

Russell Wong plays Lam Cheng Shen, a promising young lawyer, who falls in love with an exuberant young woman, Sung Neng Yee, with a mind and will of her own.

James Shigeta and France Nuyen star as Dr. and Mrs. Sung, who try to cope first with the invading Japanese and then the Chinese Communists, in the feature film *China Cry*, starring Julia Nickson-Soul as their daughter Sung Neng Yee, seen here as a child, played by Lau Lee Foon.

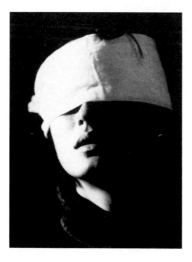

Sung Neng Yee (Julia Nickson-Soul) is blindfolded and brought before a firing squad in a scene from *China Cry*.

Dennis Chan plays a university professor in *China Cry*.

A firing squad takes aim at Sung Neng Yee in a scene from the feature film, *China Cry*.

Russell Wong and Julia Nickson-Soul are the stars of *China Cry* a feature film detailing a true, intimate love story set in Mainland China.

The feature film *China Cry* is based on the early life of Nora Lam. Lam escaped from Mainland China to Hong Kong, coming to the United States in 1966.

12

A SEARING LIGHT

I stared at my interrogator in shock.

Surely, she meant this as another threat to frighten me.

But no. I could see it in her eyes; she was completely mad with anger. Her jaw muscles tremored, her eyes blazed with hate, foam dribbled down her chin.

"Take her out and shoot her!" she screamed again. "That's an *order*."

The two soldiers, who seemed frozen with unbelief, suddenly jerked to life. Grabbing my arms, they turned, yanked me out the room, and dragged me down a hallway.

In panic, I tried to break away, screaming, "No! No! I am pregnant. You cannot kill two of us."

Nausea filled me and bile rose in my throat. I stumbled and lost my footing. The soldiers mindlessly continued hauling me like a sack of grain. My slippers fell off, and for an instant I remembered the old man I had seen in downtown Shanghai dragged to the police car, leaving his shoes behind.

They pushed a door open, and we were out in a large courtyard. A cold evening breeze chilled me. My escorts said something to an officer, who glanced at me and nodded. I felt I was sleepwalking in a nightmare.

One wall of the courtyard was pockmarked with bullet holes. I was hustled up to the brick parquet and turned around. Facing me in the dusk stood a line of soldiers, rifles at their sides. My interrogator had come out and stood near them.

A soldier yanked my arms behind my back and tied my wrists together. Another pulled a rag across my eyes and knotted it behind my head. It was all so unreal. Yet I knew that executions were happening all the time. I would be just one of many today. The evening breeze ruffled my jacket, and my baby moved within me.

The interrogator's voice called to me sardonically. "Deny your Christian God and perhaps we'll reconsider. Otherwise," she laughed hysterically, "you'll soon find out for yourself He doesn't exist."

Closer to me, a voice said, "You have two minutes. Do you have a message for your husband—your parents? It will be passed on."

I shook my head, knowing they would only use my message to persecute my family.

Tears moistened my blindfold as I thought about my baby and family. Would they be allowed to claim my body?

"One minute . . ." said the voice.

"Ready!" someone shouted. I heard rifle bolts click as bullets slid into their chambers.

"Aim!"

Though I walk through the valley of the shadow of death, I whispered, *I shall fear no evil . . . for Thou art with me . . .*

A strong gust of wind blew through the courtyard. Dust stung my face below the blindfold. I struggled to maintain my balance.

"Oh Father," I prayed . . . "Please forgive me for

my years of silence. Help my baby who has never known life outside my body . . . Help my Cheng Shen, . . . my parents . . ."

In the howl of the rising wind I could barely hear the word.

"Fire!"

Guns exploded; bullets cracked; chips of brick stung my arms and back. I collapsed onto the ground.

Was this all there was to dying?

The echo of gunfire reverberated in the night; then there was silence.

I continued lying motionless. Then I realized I was breathing. I was still alive. What had happened?

Footsteps approached. I sat up, wriggled my hands free, pulled the blindfold away. The firing squad stood staring at me, seemingly in shock, their rifles half-lowered. A soldier pulled me to my feet. I looked around. My interrogator was gone. Soldiers milled about, talking excitedly. I was dragged back into the building and pushed into a room where I slumped against the wall in shock.

I was awakened by someone shaking my shoulder. "Come with me," ordered a soldier who escorted me to a room where the official who had first questioned me sat behind a desk. He looked up at me speculatively, his hand fingering his coat collar.

"You may sit," he said.

"Thank you."

"You know," he said, "it was not my plan for you to die. An ambitious Party official collecting trophies for his dossier. These things happen. . . . As our Chairman Mao wrote: 'To right a wrong, it is necessary to exceed the proper limits . . .'"

"Yes, I know," I answered numbly, thinking of the many who had died in exceeding "proper limits."

"But I felt the light . . . the warmth," I said, still dazed. "Bullets struck the wall all around me."

He shook his head. "It has been determined that it was some form of electrical disturbance. A freak windstorm."

"Colonel, I respectfully request to speak to someone who was there. Perhaps one of the soldiers?"

"To what purpose?" he asked sharply.

"I would like to ask . . ."

He smiled. "If they observed a lightning bolt from heaven?" He laughed. "Why would the Christian God create a miracle for you? Since you did not claim Him for such a long time?"

"Perhaps He remembers more than our minds can hold."

He stared at me for a moment, as if struggling with something, then composing himself, he suddenly stood up.

"That's all," he snapped. "You are hereby notified by the People's Republic that you have been released from your teaching position." He turned to an attendant soldier. "Take her away."

Lesser party officials grilled me in ensuing days. There were more screaming accusations, more probing questions, more slappings and cursings. But somehow I now felt inured to it all. As if Someone else were taking care of me. I thought of the Old Man who used to come and visit me as a little girl. I knew now Who had taken his place.

One night He spoke to me. Thrown into a guarded room for the night, I slept soundly. And, as if I were in a dream, a Voice sounded: *Do not be afraid, My child. The day will come when you and all your family will get out of Red China.*

I awoke with joy surging through me.

In a few days I was allowed to go home. But I didn't tell Cheng Shen or my father about the firing squad. Both were already so persecuted they seemed near the breaking point. I did tell Mother, hoping it would encourage her that God, indeed, had worked a miracle.

She took me in her arms and held me close, rocking me back and forth as she had when I was a baby.

"Mother," I looked up at her. "After my miraculous deliverance from the firing squad, God promised me in a dream that our whole family will escape from Red China. We all will be *free*. Isn't that wonderful?"

She smiled wistfully and shook her head. It was too much for her to believe.

It was increasingly difficult for me to believe, too, after I returned to my school. Though I was no longer permitted to teach, I was not forgotten. Day after day I was forced to write my life story, telling everything I had ever known about my parents, relatives, friends, and teachers. What they thought about Communism, who their friends were.

When each page was finished I had to stamp my fingerprints on it to prove the words were mine. But nothing I wrote satisfied my persecutors.

"It's too short!"

"It's not clear."

"Obviously not true."

And then: "Write it all again . . . from the beginning. Don't pretend you don't know. Tell everything."

They never let me keep a copy of what I had written because they wanted to find inconsistencies to trap me at the next interrogation session.

In between writing my life story, I would be dragged into a large room and put under a spotlight for questioning.

One after another, interrogators lashed me with questions, threatening to kill my loved ones if I didn't give them the answers they wanted.

Then I was surprised to find myself in a small, comfortably furnished room with a friendly-faced man sitting across from me. "Now my dear, I understand how difficult this is for you," he soothed. "And believe me, I am the last one to want to see you suffer. I want to be your friend."

Gently, insidiously, he would try to lead me into making a confession, or, worse, betraying a friend.

When I didn't respond, I was dragged back to face my brutal questioners. And I wondered, which was the more cruel, the ones who were open about their evil, or the one who hid behind a gentle mask?

I worried about the effect this was having on my unborn child. As I prayed, I told the baby within me that God loved him and cared for him.

Ever so often the Party officials would allow me to go home. Usually, only Mother would be there. For Cheng Shen and Father often had to spend the night away, Father at the factory clinic, Cheng Shen at his court.

They, too, would be questioned. On one rare night when Cheng Shen was home, he sighed, "They questioned me last night, again."

"Oh, Cheng Shen," I mourned, laying my head against his chest. "I know how painful that can be."

He gave a short laugh. "You won't believe what it was about."

I looked at him questioningly.

"All about the nylons I brought you from Hong Kong, and our first date; the concert, remember?"

"You mean . . . ?"

"Yes, I had to explain exactly what I had given you, why I chose that particular restaurant, even where I bought my phonograph records, and . . . and they wanted to know why my father had so many concubines."

Cheng Shen laughed bitterly, his eyes looking far away. "They wanted to know if my father shared them with me."

He slammed his hand on the table. "I don't know how much longer I can take this so-called People's Republic."

I stroked his forehead, wondering if I should tell him what God had told me. But our child moved within me again; I placed his hand on my stomach and whispered. "There, Cheng Shen, you can feel our future."

A few days later on the night of February 14, 1956, I was awakened by labor pains. A pedicab took me to the hospital where a doctor examined me and gruffly noted, "First babies take a long time." He rushed off to other patients and left me sitting in a chair in a cold hallway all night. Finally, a bed was found. By then I was nearly unconscious with pain. I awakened enough to see my mother wiping the perspiration from my face.

"Cheng Shen?" I gasped. "Where is he?"

"I told you," she said. "They keep him at the People's Court, sometimes until late at night. Try to rest. The doctor predicts a difficult passage."

Another day went by. Blood soaked the bedclothes. On my third day of labor, a nurse said, "The baby's head seems too large for your birth canal. The doctor planned a Caesarean, but it is too late to do that now."

"What *can* be done?" I gasped. She shrugged, and turned away to other patients.

Finally, frantic that my baby have a chance to live, I exerted all my strength, and with a mighty tearing and rending pain, I literally forced the baby from my body.

"It's a boy," I heard someone say through my haze, "a healthy, well-formed child."

Hot tears flooded my cheeks as I silently thanked God for His miracle. In that moment, I gave my son to God, and then I slept.

When it was time to leave the hospital, Cheng Shen came to get me and our little son, whom we named Chuin Man meaning "Little scholar."

The sun was warm, a fresh breeze ruffled the leaves,

and as we climbed into the pedicab, Cheng Shen suggested, "Why don't we just ride around the city for days and *rest!*"

I laughed, holding my son close to me. "Why not fifty-six days, the official leave the government gives new mothers after childbirth?"

"All right then," he grinned, and called to the pedicab driver. "Just drive around the city for fifty-six days."

The driver glanced back over his shoulder puzzled, then caught on and laughed. The sound made me feel good; at least people could still laugh in Communist China.

I turned to Cheng Shen. "May I ask you a private question?"

"This is about as private as Shanghai gets," he smiled, "but go ahead; today, the mother of my son may ask anything!"

"Do you still believe in God?"

"God? You mean in the Christian sense?"

I nodded.

He stared out past the pedicab driver and said quietly, "Mao cut out His tongue years ago."

I squeezed his arm. "I still hear His voice."

"In the wind, no doubt."

But I was too happy to argue. "Let's walk!" I declared impulsively. "I can do it. Let's walk in the park. I want Chuin Man to see flowers and green grass."

"Do you think he'll remember?" smiled Cheng Shen.

"Yes, I think he will. Besides, we can be alone. I want to share my heart."

After that beautiful day, time fairly flew. Cheng Shen was able to be home with me more than usual.

One afternoon there was pounding on the door. I opened it to find a soldier in his green and red uniform. I almost screamed, then caught myself. He handed me an envelope, and left.

I opened it and cried out to Mother, who was giving little Chuin Man a bath on the table.

"I only have six more days, Mother. They want me back. And my milk is beginning to dry up. I must find milk for Chuin Man. What can I do?"

She looked up in concern. "Yes, when you go back to that awful place, he will be screaming for you in an hour."

I was in panic. I had not thought about leaving Chuin Man at home. But I knew under no circumstances would I bring him to that place which was a daily hell.

"Mother, I am going to try the city stores. Somehow, somewhere I'll find some milk."

Taking Chuin Man, I left the house and waited until a city bus groaned up. It was jammed with people but I luckily found a place to stand where little Chuin Man hungrily nuzzled me.

"Oh, Father," I prayed silently, "help me find milk for my baby."

As I prayed, I did not know that He was using this very emergency to introduce me to an unexpected revelation.

13

HE GIVETH AND TAKETH

It happened at a bus transfer point.

As I shuffled forward in a long line of people to buy a ticket for downtown, Chuin Man cried in my arms. I crooned a little lullaby I remembered from the Mary Farnham Mission School and looked up to see I had reached the transportation clerk. She was a gray-haired woman in her early fifties.

"Boy or girl?" she asked, not unkindly. "Your first? How old?"

"Seven weeks," I replied a bit impatiently. "A boy, and yes, my first."

"You seem worried about leaving him so soon."

I puzzled at her discernment, then replied. "He needs milk. I don't know when I can be with him. The stores in our district have been out for weeks."

The woman leaned forward and said quietly. "I know of a book that can be as nourishing to the spirit as milk for a baby."

"Unfortunately, he can't *read*," I replied, irritated. "Please, have you heard of a store that might have milk? I'll go *anywhere!*"

"My shift ends in twenty minutes," she said. "Wait for me. We'll talk about the milk."

I stood at the side of the building for what seemed to be an eternity, rocking Chuin Man in my arms. Then the woman appeared. "Come with me," she said. We hurried through a street market, vendors hawking live ducks, yams, teas. The fresh clean aroma of fruits and vegetables was pleasant.

My guide noted quietly, "We meet on market days. No one pays attention." She pushed me to a small wooden door in a stucco wall and knocked three times. A man pulled it open, the woman nodded toward me, and he quickly ushered us in. About a dozen people of all ages sat on the ground around a small table. An older man with long white hair was perched on a stool at the table. We were between two buildings, and a netting spread between them served as a canopy, filtering out the hot sun yet still allowing a warm illumination. But what struck me was the glow that seemed to come from the people. After my guide and I sat down, the pastor started speaking: "Since our time is short," he said in a thin, but strong voice, "let us speak of our Lord!"

An elderly woman with no teeth and ragged jacket raised her hand. "He is the light of the world!" she proclaimed.

Murmurs of approval rose around me. Then, a young man carefully extracted a scrap of paper from his jacket pocket and reverently placed it on the table. "I copied this from a brother who carries it in his heart," he said.

The pastor smoothed it out and holding it some distance from his eyes, read: "The Lord is my light and my salvation; whom shall I fear?"

I leaned forward; the word "light" stirred something within me.

"The Lord is the strength of my life," continued the pastor, "of whom shall I be afraid?"

Again, I found myself reliving the piercing incandescence that penetrated my blindfold; the rifles' roar echoed in my mind. I clutched Chuin Man, who whimpered in his sleep.

"The Scriptures tell us that we are 'children of the light,'" continued the pastor. "We see and hear what our tongues cannot always speak." He touched his head and his heart. "Let us offer our silent praise. What shall we sing?"

The young man called softly, "Take My Life and Let It Be."

Emotions whirled within me. It was the very hymn we sang at the Mary Farnham School!

The pastor nodded, raised his arm, and brought it down.

I started to sing "Take my life and . . ." Suddenly, I realized I was the only one singing. I looked around the room to see everyone moving their lips silently, forming the words of the hymn.

I realized. It would be dangerous if our voices were heard in the street. I "sang" along with them, "Take my life and let it be, consecrated Lord, to Thee. . . ."

The "singing" ended with a mouthed "Amen." Then the woman who brought me spoke up: "Our sister is being criticized by the authorities. She has urgent need for milk for her son."

The other women looked at me sympathetically.

The elderly one raised her hand. "I can bring fresh milk from the country every Wednesday."

"But she must have powdered milk too," said a young woman. "Carrying it so far, the milk can sour."

A middle-aged woman with glasses spoke up. "All powdered milk is exported. But my friend works in the government store. I will speak to her."

I looked around the room in amazement. Never had I heard such an outpouring on behalf of a stranger.

A few days later I again joined the long line of people shuffling forward to buy tickets at the transfer center.

When I reached the clerk, she looked around, then pushed a package across the counter with my ticket. "You forgot this last night," she said loudly, "try to remember your belongings."

"Oh, thank you," I murmured.

"Don't be so careless next time," she called as I hurried away.

Within the hour I was back home crying, "Mother! We have milk. *Powdered milk!*"

Heartened by the compassion of fellow believers, I returned to the school—or prison, as it was becoming more known to me—and walked toward the office to report in. The military students, who had once been so respectful, stepped aside and averted their faces as if I were a leper.

In the office, the colonel twirled a pencil in his hand as I stood before him. "Your son has been born at a propitious time," he said. "He has the opportunity to be ideologically pure—a true Marxist!" He looked up at me, his face somber. "All measures must be taken to assure us that he will grow up without the corruption of the past."

I was too broken, too tired to be careful with my words.

"If you are referring to the 'evils' of capitalism, Colonel, that should not be difficult. My fear is that he will grow up mindless."

The colonel's face froze, his hand closed on the pencil until it snapped.

"A more pertinent question might be," he said evenly, "if he will have parents or be assigned to a state orphanage!"

My heart chilled.

"Do you have further comment . . . . *Comrade?*"

I bowed my head in submission.

"Today," he said, rising from his desk, "you will write the history of your husband."

"But Colonel, with respect, I'm not that acquainted with his personal history."

He led me to the desk where I had spent so many previous hours writing every facet of my family's history. "But," he said, "you certainly can remember conversations with him."

He placed paper and pen before me. "Recall for us every conversation from your first meeting." He tapped the paper. "There is particular interest in the money deposited each month in your account from Hong Kong."

I looked up at him in surprise. So now they even knew everyone's banking transactions?

"But it is a small amount," I argued. "A few yuans. It comes from his family in Hong Kong. How else would we survive? My teaching salary is gone. We have become nonpersons."

He smiled. "Yes, I can see you are an observer of human nature, Comrade. The mind is a great storehouse. Write down everything!"

After several days they allowed me a night with my baby. I found a pedicab driver who was going home on his bicycle, and he let me ride on the back of it. It was late in the evening when I finally reached our hovel. Mother met me at the door.

"Your son screamed himself to sleep," she said, nodding to his crib.

"I know . . . and my milk has dried up, Mother."

"Thank your friends, for the powdered milk," she sighed.

I stepped over to a darkened corner where Chuin Man slept behind a sheet. I pulled it back to see my husband sitting by the crib, head in hands, staring at his son.

"Oh, Cheng Shen," I softly exclaimed, "I so miss seeing you. I measure each second we are alone."

"Yes, they let me go tonight," he sighed. "For once they seemed tired of questioning me." He crossed to our bed and removed his slippers. Looking at Chuin Man, he said: "He will have no childhood."

"Cheng Shen," I put my hand on his arm. "I have a plan."

He rose from the bed and clasped his hand over my mouth so hard I was frightened.

"Don't tell me *anything*, Neng Yee," he exclaimed. "They compare our stories. We must keep a low profile—we'll live longer."

We both lay down on the small bed. Moonlight from a small window flooded the room. Cheng Shen turned and looked at me.

"My husband," I whispered, "they have not cut out God's tongue."

He was silent.

"I know that to be certain," I continued. "He will hear my prayer for you."

He took me in his arms. "I am ready to lie," he groaned. "Today I was tempted to give them what they want. To let them win . . . so that I can lose. Then it will be over."

"Oh, Cheng Shen," I soothed, kissing him. "Let's remember the good things. Remember our first date?

"I can still see you sitting across from me in that restaurant," I whispered. "I can still hear you playing the piano in that club . . . I can still sense you that night in your apartment. . . ."

He pulled me close to him and asked softly, "How did we ever find each other?"

"I knew you were mine the first time I saw you on campus," I sighed, kissing him fiercely.

The next day I was back at my desk, a soldier posted at my side to make sure I continued my "confession." *They bent us like saplings in the wind,* I murmured to myself, thinking of the previous night with Cheng Shen. *Our separations are more eloquent than our meetings . . . I wonder will we ever again dare to be graceful together.*

"*Write.*" The command jolted me out of my reverie. The soldier motioned to the paper.

"What is your family name?" I asked him brightly. "We meet so often it only seems polite."

He stared at the floor impassively.

I wrote and wrote. Finally, for relaxation, I tried addressing the soldier again. "I'm sure the colonel would approve of our speaking. It occurred to me this morning that if my parents had been farmers, I might be Dean of Soochow University by now." I laughed.

My joke obviously fell flat.

I learned not to be lighthearted with my captors again. Drab weeks passed into drab months. Before long I was expecting my second child. It was hard to think of bringing another baby into this life of misery and wretched trials. There was never enough for us to eat. Our family was rationed only one small bottle of oil each month. One person had to make do with four ounces of meat and twenty pounds of rice for the same period.

On February 15, 1957, almost a year to the day my son was born, our daughter came into the world. She was a lovely baby. Again I had my fifty-six days stipulated leave, about the only thing for which I was grateful to the Communists. For now if I wasn't writing a detailed "confession" at school, I was doing menial labor.

But I wasn't to enjoy those fifty-six days of peace and freedom.

About a month after Chuin Way joined us, Father began coughing more than usual. The freezing winds and rains of winter seemed to find their way into every crack of our hovel and he came down with a bad case of influenza.

What made him especially susceptible was the continuing persecution he suffered at his work. One night he had staggered through the door and fell exhausted onto the bed. We learned that he had been summoned to a "political" meeting where he was forced to stand on a small chair for almost one day while they grilled him.

"Why was your father so wealthy?" "Why did you study in France?" "Why did you associate with Catholics?"

A few days later Father took critically ill and was hospitalized.

I rushed to the hospital and was surprised to find him in a private room.

"Papa," I cried, hugging him, "you had to get sick so we could have a visit. Very smart! And they are treating you like a big shot. A private room for a flu patient."

He placed a thin hand on mine. "Private for a reason," he whispered. Then brightening: "How is your mother?"

"Worrying about you. Never letting your grandson and granddaughter out of her sight. You know Mother."

"Neng Yee," he said seriously, "promise that you will take care of her."

"Oh, you'll be home soon, Father. It's only the flu. A couple of injections and you'll be fine."

The day came when his fever was gone, and we talked about what we'd do when he returned home.

"It will be so wonderful for all of us just to sit and talk." I said. "I have a few weeks of maternity leave left and maybe we could even visit the park."

He smiled wanly. "Even for a day; if I could only be out of here for one day."

I puzzled at his comment. And then one night when I stayed at his bedside he confided that the medical staff were testing a new medicine on him. "A day after they started I began bleeding from the bowels." He raised himself on his elbow and said weakly. "A Communist doctor—we once worked together at the Hwa Tung Textile—told me the truth. The new drug they used on me causes extensive bleeding from the bowels."

"Oh no, Father," I exclaimed. "Let me speak to the doctors about it." I rose to leave, and he took hold of my arm. "Please . . ." he shook his head weakly, "it will do no good, but will only make matters worse."

He pulled me down beside him. "I want you to remember something, Neng Yee. If you ever have more trouble than you can bear, remember you can always go to America. Many of those round-eyed black and white people are Christians. They will love you."

"Yes, Dad," I said to satisfy his concern. "And if that time comes, I have it on good authority we'll all be there together."

As I left the hospital that morning, Mother came in to take my place. I kissed her and headed home to sleep. But as I walked into our door, the phone was ringing. It was Mother.

"They stopped me before I could go into his room," she said. "They said your father is critical."

My brother Neng Yao and I rushed to the hospital. When the three of us walked into Father's room, a sheet had already been drawn up over him. I pulled it back and to my horror saw that his sheets were drenched with blood.

"He didn't die," I gasped. "He was murdered!"

A bitter wind tore at my slacks and jacket as Cheng Shen and I stood in the cemetery holding little Chuin Way. My Mother cradled one-year-old Chuin Man, and my 10-year-old brother stood with us. As they lowered Father's simple pine casket into its grave, bitter thoughts flooded me. *The crime was murder, but without proof of intent. We have to take what happens. Swallow the bitterness. Only the babies can give*

Mother life now. They will keep her from joining us as non-persons.

Then a grievous question struck me. *Oh, Father, You promised that all of our family would escape Red China. What happened?*

I did not know that in time I would be given the answer.

14

AND THEN WE WERE TWO

The rice bowl came flying from across the room to shatter on the wall behind me. If I hadn't ducked, it would have hit me. I looked up with tears in my eyes: "Please, Cheng Shen," I begged, "*please* get hold of yourself!"

My husband's eyes were wild as he picked up a dish and began to hurl it, then he slowly let his arm fall, collapsed on a chair, and began crying. I went over and put my arm around him, feeling his shoulders shake with sobs.

More and more lately, Cheng Shen had been flying into violent rages. I attributed it to the persecution he had been undergoing at the court where he worked. "Why are your parents in Hong Kong so wealthy?" "How much smuggling have you done?" They persisted.

Yet, I couldn't help but be reminded of my initial misgivings when I first met him, his bleak moods, his separating himself from others. But I had brushed those thoughts aside then, and I did it now. No, I told myself, it was the persecution he was suffering from.

In the meantime I found myself turning more and more to the Lord, realizing more than ever we all would have to leave Red China, or there would be nothing left of any of us. As a current saying went: "The long pole gets sawed off." And the Lams were a long pole.

"Please Lord," I prayed, "my father is gone, Mother isn't well, my husband is being persecuted, and I can't get enough food for my babies. Please help us escape."

Would you believe Me for one thing, He answered.

"Yes, Lord, for what?"

Trust Me for only one day at a time. If you really believe Me, you must send your daughter to your mother-in-law in Hong Kong.

It was unthinkable!

But the Lord has ways of convincing one.

Later that week I was in the house church to which I had been introduced by the transportation clerk. It was good to be there, to be able to worship openly and freely.

I settled back against the building wall trying to filter out the clamoring din of the street market outside to catch the words.

"Not all of us will escape the fire unscathed," said the pastor in his thin high voice. "Some of us will stumble so that we can be refined—purified for His purpose."

For some reason he seemed to be speaking to me. "The path of every Christian has been marked by God," he continued. Then, he pulled a scrap of paper from his pocket, unfolded it, and said, "The psalmist wrote these words: 'In God I have put my trust.' "

I looked around, impressed by how much the little congregation had grown; there were some twenty-five worshippers present.

" 'I will not be afraid of what man can do to me,' " he read, " 'for Thou hast delivered my soul from death, so that I may walk before God in the light of the living.' "

The people murmured their agreement. Then an el-

derly woman in a threadbare jacket rose to speak. In the way
she got up, I could see she was blind.

"When you plant melon seeds, you harvest melons,"
she said.

"When you plant bean seeds, you get beans.

"When you plant seeds of faith, you find God!"

The assembly nodded enthusiastically. I felt so much
at home with fellow believers I found myself standing up to
speak.

"I . . . I want to thank you for helping my babies
with the powdered milk," I said, "and for encouraging me."

The elderly pastor nodded and turned to the rest of
the people. "This is our sister of the firing squad," he announced.

I was shocked. How did he know . . . ? There were
whispers among the worshippers, many of them nodding to
each other.

"China has seen many things that some would call
'miracles' since the Revolution," he continued, "and He has
given me a message for our sister."

He looked straight at me. "Our Lord asks you to trust
Him for one day at a time."

I stood looking at him, mesmerized by his message. It
was the very same direction God had given me earlier!

"The days will become weeks, weeks . . . months,
and the months will fall into years . . . *one day at a time,*"
he emphasized.

I *knew* as he spoke this was the confirmation of God's
message.

The pastor started to continue, "And He will . . ."
when the wooden street door exploded open. In rushed
soldiers with their rifles at the ready. Worshippers screamed
and scattered like rabbits before hounds. The soldiers viciously
clubbed people right and left as they advanced through the
assembly.

An officer stood in the center of the area, raised his pistol, and fired a shot for attention. In the shocked silence that followed, he shouted:

"This is an unauthorized meeting! Line up against the wall, identity cards out!"

The elderly blind woman who had so enthusiastically spoke about "seeds of faith" groped helplessly, trying to find the wall. A soldier viciously kicked her in the bottom, sending her sprawling.

"Be calm, please be calm," cried the pastor who had raised his hands in the air. Another soldier slammed him in the stomach with his rifle butt. The elderly pastor slowly sank to his knees, a sick look of surprise on his pale face.

In the melee I found myself on my hands and knees crawling, to where I did not know, except I didn't want to stand for fear of being kicked in the stomach. I was five months pregnant with my third child.

As I crawled I felt someone grasp my arm. I looked to see the transportation clerk who had originally befriended me.

"Come," she hissed, "there is a way!"

In the confusion, no one saw us crawl behind an upended table against the stucco wall. Behind it was a hole in the masonry. The clerk pushed me through it and followed. We found ourselves in an herb shop, the proprietor studiously not noticing us as we climbed to our feet and stumbled out into the market.

As I bicycled home, my heart throbbing, I decided it would be as God directed. I would trust Him for one thing at a time, one day at a time. He had directed me to send my baby daughter, Chuin Way, to her grandmother in Hong Kong, and I would do it.

As it happened so often, when I obeyed God, everything seemed to fall into place. Cheng Shen agreed that it was best. "I know my mother would love to have her," he said, "she is always writing asking for snapshots of her grandchildren."

We also had a friend, a nanny, Yee Ah Hsing, who was going to Hong Kong. Ah Hsing said she would be happy to take Chuin Way with her.

I applied for their exit permits and expected the usual interminable wait, the innumerable questions, and tangle of red tape.

Three weeks later, the permits came; I was amazed.

However, even though I knew it was right in the Lord's eyes, saying goodbye to my daughter was more than I could bear. So I accompanied Chuin Way and her nanny as far as I could. For two days and three nights the three of us rode on the train to Canton. It was hot and crowded but I didn't mind; it gave me that much more time to cuddle my daughter, who smiled up at me.

But the worst moment came at the Canton pier where the nanny and Chuin Way would board a steamer for Macao, the port city from where they would travel to Hong Kong.

A gray salty mist drifted in from the South China Sea, and droplets of moisture collected on Chuin Way's little woolen coverlet. As travelers surged around us heading for the gangplank, I held my daughter close, not wanting to give her up. She must have sensed we were going to part because she placed her little arms around my neck and clung tightly. Finally, I handed her to Ah Hsing who quickly turned and hurried up the gangplank.

I felt as if I were losing part of me. Suddenly I looked up to see Ah Hsing with Chuin Way standing before me. She handed me a tiny gold cross that had hung around my daughter's neck.

"I have to return it," she said. "The Communists will not permit anyone to take gold out of the country." I took it, kissed Chuin Way again, and watched them disappear in the gray mist.

I did not remember the long, lonely train trip home. I was too numb with grief. I sat gripping my daughter's little gold cross in my hand all the way. The only thing that sustained me was knowing I was following God's will.

Shortly after I returned home I faced a sorrow even more heartrending. I found Cheng Shen in deep despair standing by our little window looking out into the crowded alley. At first I thought he was in one of his dark moods, and I dared not disturb him. For these would often pass in a few hours, and we'd be talking again as husband and wife.

But this time it was different.

"Word came to me today," he said quietly, "that they are planning to assign me to a labor camp."

I jumped up and cried, "No, no, they can't!" We had all heard about the labor camps. The labor was so excruciating that even men in good health died. And Cheng Shen who had suffered from tuberculosis as a child had never been strong. One of his brothers in Hong Kong was already dying from the same disease. If Cheng Shen had to go to a labor camp I knew he would never survive.

"But all educated people should have experience at hard labor," my husband said sardonically, parroting the common maxim of the Communist leaders.

He turned from the window and gathered me in his arms. "Neng Yee, I knew it was coming to this. For two years now they have been making it hard for me at the court. After all," he laughed bitterly, "anyone from a wealthy Hong Kong family with a good education must be considered a potential traitor. So I am not surprised. I am just happy that we have had these years together."

He touched my swollen belly gently. "He—or she— will be born when I am gone. But perhaps I will see my third child one day."

I buried my face in Cheng Shen's shoulder weeping. Suddenly, I backed away and looked him in the eye.

"You are *not* going to a labor camp, Cheng Shen," I said resolutely. "You are going to Hong Kong!"

His mouth hung open. "What . . . what do you mean?"

"I will write your mother . . ."

"But what can she do?"

"I don't exactly know," I said, puzzling. But deep within me it was as if God were telling me this was the second step He had planned.

That night I wrote Cheng Shen's mother about her son's danger. "I would rather have your son live with you in Hong Kong than have him stay with me and die in a labor camp," I wrote.

Her answer was something of a miracle. Cheng Shen's father, she wrote, was actually critically ill with a liver disease; his doctors did not expect him to live very long.

I showed the letter to the officer who held jurisdiction over Cheng Shen. "You'll note my mother-in-law has enclosed a certificate signed by the doctor," I said, standing before his desk. "I respectfully request a thirty-day exit permit for my husband to visit his father at this time of sadness."

"Hmmmm," he sniffed, studying the letter. "A disease of the liver . . . Even rich men cannot buy off death." He looked up at me suspiciously. "But doctors can be made to sign anything for a price, especially in Hong Kong," he snorted.

"Besides," he added, pushing the letter back at me, "your husband has been assigned to a camp where he will experience labor reform. All educated people should know how to work with their backs."

"Please, sir," I begged. "Could this order not be post-poned for thirty days?"

"How do you know he won't abandon you?"

"I have his son," I said. "Family ties remain important

even in the new China. And," I added, feeling a blush warm my neck and face, "I am pregnant."

Again, as if in verification of God's promise, and despite everything pointing to the contrary, an exit permit was issued within a week. Out of all the men working in Cheng Shen's court system who wanted to get out of Red China at that time, my husband was the only one who received permission to go.

I packed his clothes and Chuin Man and I went to the railroad station to bid him farewell. We sadly walked into the clamoring station with its hissing engines and clouds of steam, *Why*, I wondered, *were railroad stations always a scene of sadness for me?* First my family's long trip to Chungking, then taking my daughter Chuin Way to Canton, and now, seeing my husband leave.

It was May, and flowerbeds outside the station were in fragrant bloom as we walked into the station, little Chuin Man toddling along with us. As we passed the flowers, my heart caught as I remembered that moment long ago when Cheng Shen brought me a yellow tulip on that Saturday work day at Soochow University.

Oh, how I wanted time to stand still, to grant us eternity together. Finally, we stood outside his green coach, both of us stealing glances at the clock, hoping the hands would not move.

Cheng Shen embraced me and little Chuin Man again.

"Husband," I said huskily, "be sure to send a telegram as soon as you reach Hong Kong. Stress that the family needs me there. Ask that I join you there for the birth of our baby. I will try for an exit permit, please . . . I need your approval."

Cheng Shen looked down at the station platform and shook his head sadly. "Don't be a dreamer," he sighed. "They will never let you go." He looked at me, his jaw resolute. "I *will* come back, Neng Yee, I promise you, *I will come back!*"

"No," I cried. "You must not even consider it. God will free us all. I have His promise that we will *all* get out of China. You *must* take this first step."

I looked at him pleadingly. "Touch me again, please."

The hands of the clock inexorably edged to the departure hour. The train man called out the boarding signal. Cheng Shen wrapped me again in his arms, ruffled little Chuin Man's hair, grabbed his luggage, turned, and mounted the steel steps of the coach.

The locomotive's exhaust thundered, its bell commenced clanging, pistons hissed, and the coach began moving. Cheng Shen stood in its vestibule waving at us.

Holding our son, I began hurrying along the platform keeping up with the moving coach. Acrid coal smoke choked me.

"Cheng Shen," I called through streaming tears, "I don't know if I'll see you again . . ." Steam clouds obscured him for a moment.

"I don't know if I'll see you again while I'm still in my twenties," I cried hurrying to keep up with him, "or when I'm thirty or forty . . . or fifty . . ."

The train accelerated and Cheng Shen's coach moved away from me.

"But we'll meet again someday," I called to him through the smoke and steam. *"Please*, dear husband, please wait for me."

Then he was lost in billowing clouds. I stood on the platform watching. The last coach's red warning lights blurred in my tears until they disappeared down the track.

When I returned home that night there was a call from my school telling me to report early the next morning.

They had a surprise waiting for me.

15

CLIMBING COAL MOUNTAIN

"**W**hat you need is some heavy labor," observed the officer as he sat back in his chair looking at me. With my body swollen with fluid, I weighed over 200 pounds. My kidneys and liver had become infected. He leaned forward to stamp a paper. "It will be good for you physically and will teach you that even the cultured and well-educated must work alongside the peasant for the success of the Communist cause." He glanced at my expanding girth and added, "It will be especially good for you since you are expecting a child."

He pushed the paper at me. "Take this and report each morning at 5 A.M.—Chin Lee Square."

When I told Mother, she laid face down on her cot. "We must all die, now," she cried. "You will die and so will I."

"No, Mother, remember, I have God's word. We will all get out of China." She was crying too loudly to hear.

Early the next morning with a hint of dawn in the eastern sky, I climbed wheezing and puffing into the back of a big truck jammed with other teachers and students assigned to the "re-education camp." Nauseated from my infection, I gripped the stanchion of the truck as it swerved and bounced over the rutted road, closing my eyes against the pain. When the truck ground to a stop, I opened them.

Looming against the gray morning sky was a mountain of coal over ten stories high. People who looked like ants climbed the mountain, loaded baskets, descended, pushed their baskets up over the side of waiting trucks, and climbed back up the hill again.

"Out! Out!" yelled a guard carrying a whip. As people started climbing down, they did not move fast enough to suit him. Cracking the whip, he screamed, "Hurry, pigs! You are too slow." One woman had trouble getting off the truck; reaching up he yanked her to the ground where she lay crumpled. He kicked her in the side; gasping in pain she slowly pulled herself up, holding onto the side of the truck.

Pointing his whip toward a heap of bamboo baskets and poles, he shouted, "All of you, get to work!" A guard handed me two baskets and a pole.

"But I'm pregnant," I said. The guard laughed and shoved me toward the mountain. "It will be good for you and the baby, Cow."

Joining the others, I trudged up the splintery wooden boards laid on the coal. "Do they give us shovels," I called to the bent-over man in front of me who seemed to have been working here for some time.

He turned, looked at me through red-rimmed eyes and showed me his hands; they were black with coal dust, raw and bleeding.

No one spoke; the only sound was the scraping of feet on the planks, the crack of whips and epithets screamed by the guards. At our loading point, I knelt down and scooped the acrid-smelling coal into the baskets. Slipping the yoke through their basket handles, I started to straighten up when a guard stepped over, slammed the baskets with his whip, and yelled, "More!"

I filled them to the brims, bent under the yoke and, gritting my teeth, stood up. Together the baskets weighed about 130 pounds. Then I staggered down the precarious planks to the waiting truck, spilled each basket over the side, and, gasping for breath, headed back up the mountain.

The sun was up and hot; sweat stung my eyes, and I longed for a hat. As noon approached my face burned, and every pore of my skin was filled with black dust. My body seemed to have swollen even more; each step was agony. I no longer kept count of the trips I made; now I could only place one foot before the other, kneel, fill the baskets, stand up, stagger down, lift the baskets into the truck, and do it all over again.

"Oh Lord," I prayed, "I will die before this day is done."

Do not worry, He seemed to say, *with Me you can move any mountain. I will never let you be burdened with more than you can carry.*

I lifted my head and struggled on. But by noon when we were allowed a few minutes to eat our meager ration of rice peppered with coal dust, I looked at my bleeding hands and wept.

Weeks passed; my third child was soon due. I clung to the thought of the fifty-six days maternity leave.

In the meantime, Cheng Shen had sent me the telegram asking me to join him for the birth of the baby. I would use it to apply for an exit permit.

But the local official shook his head when I showed it to him. "No. You are serving your husband's term at forced labor until he returns—to test your resolve."

Now weighing 235 pounds, I waddled out of the office in despair, made it to our home where I was allowed to spend the night, and collapsed. My spine felt like a white-hot rod. I couldn't even lie down to rest. Instead, I hunched on the floor trying to sleep.

After a few days on the coal pile, I could stand it no longer. "Lord," I cried out one night, "please release me from this suffering. I yearn to be in a land that's free. You promised . . ."

His voice was clear: *Neng Yee, I am with you. Trust Me. If I am for you, who can be against you?*

I looked up toward the ceiling. "I need a sign, Lord. It is so hard. Please give me some assurance."

As long as the baby is in your womb, I am with you. Your child will be a son, and he will not be born in Red China; he will be born in Hong Kong.

The next morning as I climbed the tortuous mountain from which wisps of smoke seeped in the blazing sun, God's promise helped sustain me.

From time to time I was ordered to the government clinic. Concern for prospective new citizens of the Republic was high, and so pregnant mothers were examined regularly. I was glad for the respite.

"I have not felt the baby moving for two days," I told the doctor.

Removing the stethoscope from his ears, he shrugged. "The heartbeat is strong. There is evidence in you of a kidney infection. That is why you retain fluids. The nurse will give you some Vitamin C tablets."

He glanced at his chart. "Could you have miscalculated your time? This is your ninth month?"

"Yes, doctor," I said, "I know it's my ninth month. But I do not worry."

He looked at me strangely and waved in the next patient.

After a few weeks I went to the Shanghai Central Police station one night to apply for my exit permit. Holding Cheng Shen's telegram in my hand and wheezing from my climb up the steps, I approached the clerk at the main desk. He was reading a newspaper and did not look up.

"Excuse me," I began. "I am here to apply for an exit permit. I intend to visit relatives in Hong Kong during my fifty-six-day maternity leave."

He glanced up from his newspaper and stared at my girth. "Ha!" he snorted, "you should have applied months ago. Your baby will be sitting up before the application gets stamped by all the official agencies."

"But will I be permitted to fill out the appropriate forms?"

He pointed to a window behind him. "The forms are easy. The procedure is difficult." He turned back to his paper.

Even filling out the forms added to my hope. Without that bit of assurance I would not have made it through my days of torture. As I climbed the pile following the older man I had talked to earlier, I noticed he was moving slower than usual. His jacket was ripped open by whip lashes. I had heard he had been a government official in the pre-Communist regime. Now he was being "re-educated."

Suddenly, he halted, then toppled over into the coal. His body slid downhill like a rag doll. As the dusty coal avalanched over it, one limp hand stuck out as if in supplication.

I crouched down, burying my face and prayed for his soul. A whip crack exploded over my head and hot pain seared my shoulder.

"Up, Cow!" roared a guard, the whip shaking in his hand, "or must I give you one again?"

I glanced back to see the guards dragging the body of the old man to a truck. They slung it in and the truck rumbled away.

Soon I was again on my knees clawing at chunks of coal. I heard a low voice. It was a woman kneeling next to me methodically filling her basket. "I hear you, too, were once a teacher," she said. "Chemistry was my subject—seventeen years."

"But we don't talk here," I said apprehensively, still feeling the sting of the whiplash.

"I know," she whispered. "But I miss intelligent conversation. They work us like animals, but what is in our minds will not go away."

I gave her a quick smile, hoisted my baskets, and picked my way down the plank. No, I thought to myself, what is in our minds will not go away, nor what is within my belly, either.

I spoke to my unborn son silently: "I am assured that you are well and waiting. Waiting was always a shallow virtue for me, little one . . . until now."

A few days later I was back in front of the clerk at the police station.

"Have you any news for Lam Neng Yee? My exit permit?"

"Yes, I have news for you," he spat sarcastically. "Go to the Bath House. You stink like a beggar!"

"I will return in two days." I snapped.

He slammed his newspaper down. "I told you! You are dreaming."

Late that night as I washed the coal dust from me, with little Chuin Man asleep, and my brother Neng Yao studying his lessons, Mother said quietly, "Your new one will be born soon."

"The baby will not be born in China, Mother."

She shook her head, having heard this before. "I don't understand why God would speak directly to you."

"Because no one else could deliver the message." I smiled.

She sighed. "I once read a book about Christian saints in the Middle Ages. They talked like you."

"I have His promise, Mother."

"Has he promised to keep you alive in that hell hole?" she asked shrilly.

Now even I was beginning to wonder.

The next morning as I lifted my coal basket to dump it in the truck, I cried out in pain.

A guard laughed, "The old cow is slowing down."

Another giggled. "That baby is going to get dumped with the coal."

It was the ridicule, plus the rising hopelessness after again going to the police station and finding no exit permit, that depressed me to the point of seeing the fortune teller.

I knew it was wrong. Father's admonition still rang in my memory. But I was weak. One night after work I went to her little alley place.

"My name is Wong Shan," I lied. "I live in Shanghai West, Row number 186, ground floor."

"Why are you here?" she asked, regarding my swollen coal-covered body suspiciously.

"I believe something that may not be true," I said. "Can you see my future?"

She tossed her sticks, and let them fall on the table. After studying them a moment, she said, "The path is closed. You must be content with your destiny."

As I stumbled home in the dark, I apologized to the Lord for seeking answers from someone else than Him. "I believe You, Father, I believe You. And I know your promise is for one day at a time."

I stopped, leaned against a tree and looked up pleadingly. "But the days are like talons, tearing at my heart."

The next morning as I got off the truck, a guard ordered me to report to the medical section. There, after examining me, the doctor droned to a clerk who took down his notes: "The patient is twenty six years old, sentenced to hard labor . . . loads coal ten hours a day, seven days a week. Her baby's vital signs appear normal. Yet this is the three hundred sixty-second day of her pregnancy."

He looked up at me and grunted, "Hard labor seems

to agree with the baby. He moves up and down but not out. One would think you came from peasant stock."

"He must be waiting for something!" I answered.

But for what? I wondered that night bouncing on the truck. As I climbed down from the tailgate, I fell and rolled to protect my child.

"Get rid of that baby!" yelled a guard. "By now it will be a mental case!"

I didn't even look at him as I got up and started toward the telegraph office. I had my mind made up. Inside the open-all-night agency, I wrote on the message form and handed it to the clerk.

"Where do you want this to go?"

"To our great Chairman Mao Tse-tung. To Zhou En Lai, Vice Minister of Foreign Affairs, and the Central Police in Beijing."

The clerk read my message back to me to confirm it:

"You won't let me go! I am using my fifty-six days maternity leave to go so it will not interfere with my labor training job. You have no reason not to grant me an exit permit. Please check with other departments to see what they are doing with my application."

The clerk drew a deep breath and looked up at me. "It is over twenty-one words. You lose the economy rate." Then she exclaimed: "You want to send *three* telegrams to Beijing, each fifty words?"

"I have cash," I said. "Let me check your count. Every word is important." I handed her money I had gotten from selling a few pieces of my parent's furniture.

She took it shaking her head.

By now disdainful reactions from others didn't bother me, not even when I returned to the central police station and the clerk grimaced: "You again! Don't ask! Just go."

"Why is it in Shanghai," I retorted angrily, "nobody has any answers. So I have to go to the top of the ladder!"

He sneered. "Go wherever you want, Crazy One, as long as it's *away* from here!"

I had nowhere else to go but to the coal mountain. The hot sun of summer had cracked my skin open. In the hundred-degree heat and high humidity I could only close my eyes against the stinging sweat and walk the wooden planks, putting one foot before the other.

The chemistry teacher whispered at me as we filled our baskets. "How can you find the strength?"

I didn't even have the strength to answer. But I did find the strength late at night to go to the telegraph office and send another wire.

The clerk read the message and asked me incredulously: "You want Chairman Mao to check on the Vice Minister of Foreign Affairs?"

"Yes, and the Beijing Police . . . ninety-seven words!"

I left the office stepping out into the night. I felt a cool evening breeze blowing from the river, leaned against the building, and breathed gratefully, "Thank You, Father, when I can go no further, You send me refreshment. I trust You, Father, but You should know, instead of one day at a time, I now go one footstep at a time."

A week later that special Tuesday dawned like any other day. A rooster crowed somewhere down our alley, and I awakened to already feel the oppressive heat of August closing in on me. I was twelve months pregnant and I groaned as I got out of bed.

That morning I had to go to my former school to clear up some papers before reporting to the labor camp. As I waited in the school office, I heard from Him. A faint whisper inside, but I knew it was Him.

Neng Yee. The way is now open for you to get out of Red China.

After leaving the school, I rushed to the phone to tell

Mother, then headed to the labor camp. By the time I reached the towering black mountain I began to have doubts. Was my promise just wishful hearing?

Balancing the yoke with its baskets on my back, I slowly started up the splintered plank. A whistle shrieked.

"You there! The fat one. Come back."

I turned, saw a guard motioning to me, and picked my way down past hollow-eyed people slowly climbing up.

The guard motioned toward an empty truck. "They want you at the central police station! Get in."

Now what? I wondered. *Was I going to be imprisoned for daring to complain to the Chairman of the People's Republic of China?* In the bouncing truck I leaned into the wind to dry the sweat on my face, too exhausted to care what would happen.

At the police station the all-too-familiar clerk motioned me past him. "The chief wants to see you," he said in a bored tone. "For the life of me, I can't understand why."

I headed to the office he pointed out, knocked, and stepped in.

The man sitting behind the desk was seething with anger.

"I was told you looked like a beggar," he snapped. He stood up, his mustache quivering as he spoke. "It's bad enough that you use that old trick of maternity leave. In fifty-six days you could go around the world."

For some reason all fear left me. "Then I would be back in Shanghai, sir."

He turned white, then composed himself. "Eh, cunning like a beggar, too." He walked over to the window and looked out, continuing to speak. "Have you any idea how much trouble your telegrams have given us?" He swung around and said. "Beijing has called us twice about your application. This office has been unduly criticized! You have caused us to lose face."

"I only seek what is right," I said quietly. So, I thought, my telegrams *had* some effect.

"You are bad luck," he fairly shrieked. "Honest labor has affected your brain!"

"Quite possible, sir."

With a look of disgust, he threw a paper at me. I stooped to pick it up and when I saw what it was, I stared at him in unbelief. It was my exit permit.

"Usually we take steps to ensure that someone who leaves our country returns," he snapped. "But in *your* case, we demand that you *get out* . . . and *stay* out!"

"Only God knows if I'll return, sir," I said. "China is my home."

"Please take your God with you!" he screamed. "Tell him it is His last chance to escape. Within a decade He will be locked away in a museum."

"To do that, sir, you would have to imprison the wind."

I turned and walked out.

As I left the building I passed the clerk reading his newspaper. "Thank you for helping me," I said sweetly. He stared at me open-mouthed.

On the way home, I stopped at our bank and got just enough money for our airline tickets from my safe-deposit box. Since I couldn't take any valuables out of the country, I left them and the rest of the money in the box for Mother. At the airline office, I bought tickets for Chuin Man and me on the next day's flight. Then I said farewell to a few close friends. One of them, Mei-an, cried saying she knew we would never see each other again. "Of course we will," I said, trying to comfort her. "Perhaps in heaven," she answered tearfully.

At home, I packed a few pieces of clothing for my son and myself, and said goodbye to my fourteen-year-old brother Neng Yao, and Mother. In the innocence of youth, Neng Yao said "I'll be seeing you, my sister." But Mother had broken down. "My darling," she cried, "I do not know how much longer I have to live. I am afraid I will never see you again." I hugged her. "You will come, Mother. I have His promise. I know we will all be together again."

Early next morning two-year-old Chuin Man and I sat glued to the airliner's window as it took off from Shanghai airport heading for Canton. I looked down at the city with early morning sunlight glancing off its buildings. Somewhere down there was my mother and brother, and my heart panged. Despite the torture, the horror of the firing squad, the terrible ordeal of the black mountain, I felt sad at leaving my home city.

Then, I settled back in my seat as the plane roared on. I relaxed in the Lord's presence, remembering His teaching about living one day at a time. I still was not out of China. And I did not know what awaited in Hong Kong. So I decided to live just one hour at a time.

It was well I did.

16

OUT OF THE FRYING PAN . . .

Red flags whipped furiously in the strong wind blowing across the Chinese border. Little Chuin Man and I stood in the outpost building tired from the long and arduous trip from the Canton airport. We had taken taxis, buses, and small boats to get here. Now we looked out at over a mile of desert wasteland which we would have to cross on foot to reach Macao. There we hoped to meet Cheng Shen and then take a boat for the final forty-five miles to Hong Kong.

The border guards carefully searched me. "This one could burst before she makes the crossing," he joked to his partner.

"Send her off quickly," the other one laughed. "Let the other side clean up the mess."

"Some water, please," I begged, "for my little boy."

"We are not your servants," snapped the first guard.

"Here," cried the other, stepping over and grabbing my hand. "You forgot something." He pulled off my wedding ring. "Gold!" he snapped. "It goes back."

"Please send it to my mother in Shanghai," I pleaded, giving him her address.

Finally, they pushed us beyond the barricade. I hesitated a moment. We were *free*. But not yet. Before us stretched a shimmering No-Man's Land. I picked up Chuin Man and started walking. But I was so physically and emotionally exhausted, that the rocky terrain wavered in my vision. The sun was like a thousand-watt lightbulb on my head, and I began stumbling. I put Chuin Man down and, holding his hand, staggered on. He hung back crying.

"Chuin Man," I gasped, "there is nothing we can do; we must go on." Pain flashed through me as I stumbled on rocks, and sharp underbrush tore at my clothes and skin.

Eyes squinting against the blazing sun, I felt as if I was on the coal pile again. "Oh Father, I need your help," I gasped. "I cannot make it."

Would I forsake you now? He seemed to answer.

I struggled on, little Chuin Man crying as I pulled him along. He was so thirsty, and my mouth was parched. The gray-yellow terrain seemed to undulate before me. It was impossible to take another step. I tried, staggered, and sprawled forward, my face in the hot dirt. I lay semi-conscious, unable to rise. Chuin Man stopped crying, and now he tugged at my arm. "Mama, get up!" he pleaded. "Mama, get *up!*"

His tiny determined tug infused me with new strength; I struggled to my knees. Looking up through the shimmering heat waves I made out the faint outline of a massive stone arch. Through the haze it appeared as a mirage. But I knew what it was. The massive Barrier Gate marking the northern limit to Macao. *Freedom!*

Thank You, Father, I prayed, for delivering us, for bringing us to this free land. From this day on, Lord, give me the grace to lift up Jesus and tell people everywhere what You have done in my life, and what You can do in theirs.

As we walked through the big gate, a hot wind was blowing but I no longer felt thirsty or tired. It seemed as if years of persecution lifted from my back. Even Chuin Man didn't cry anymore but toddled along with me, looking curiously at all the people in bright clothes instead of the drab blue Mao slacks and jackets.

Crowds thronged the streets, many waiting for loved ones making their way from Red China. Our condition seemed to touch hearts, for several people offered us food and drink.

Chuin Man gulped down several large glasses of water. Then, his bright brown eyes sparkling with pleasure, he poured one of them over his head and laughed. It was the first time I had seen him laugh in a long time.

Someone offered him an orange; he stared at it not sure what it was. Another person held out a large piece of bread. He knew what *that* was and snatched it to greedily chomp away on it.

After enjoying some cooling water and eating a bit of bread, I searched the crowd for my husband.

Then I recognized a tall young man with a woman next to him. It was Cheng Shen's brother and his wife. I remembered them from a snapshot Cheng Shen had shown me.

I walked up to them, knowing they would never recognize me, for my features were so swollen with fluids.

"Hello," I greeted. "I am Neng Yee, your brother's wife," I pointed to Chuin Man. "His eldest son."

They looked astonished. "I am deeply ashamed of my appearance," I said. "We must appear as animals."

Cheng Shen's brother bowed politely. "Oh, but we understand. My brother has explained it to us."

He spoke Cantonese and I Mandarin, so we had a difficult time communicating.

"My husband?" I asked looking around. "Where is he?"

"I am sorry. Your husband did not have the correct

papers to make the trip. We will get you to Hong Kong as quickly as we can make arrangements."

While waiting for new identification papers that would allow us to enter Hong Kong, we stayed in a hotel where my mother-in-law had sent a servant to help care for my son. I walked around the area a bit and was shocked. Where I had left a bleak land with little food, I now saw a city where gambling held full sway and people at the gaming tables could enjoy all the free food and drink they wanted. There was such an air of wantonness it seemed almost as repellent as the grueling persecution of the country I left.

We boarded a boat for Hong Kong and when Chuin Man and I stepped onto the dock in Hong Kong we faced another police inspection. I worried but it appeared my father-in-law's money had paved the way, and we were quickly approved for entry.

I eagerly looked over the crowd of people waiting for disembarking passengers. There he was: Cheng Shen! My heart leaped, as it did when I first saw him striding across the university campus seven years ago. I rushed and threw my arms around him. I knew it wasn't seemly to demonstrate affection in public, but this time I didn't care.

Cheng Shen, though a bit taken aback, seemed glad to see me. He turned and pointed to two Rolls Royces and a Mercedes full of people. "Some of my family and other relatives," he said sheepishly. "They wanted to welcome you."

All were prosperous looking, men in dark business suits and women in long silk gowns. I felt ashamed of my size and poor clothes.

We entered one of the limousines; Cheng Shen spoke to the chauffeur, and we glided through Hong Kong. I was amazed by the huge, tall skyscrapers. Finally, we approached the Lam residence, driving past two stern-looking stone lions guarding the entry way, and pulling to a stop before an ornate three-story mansion of old Chinese architecture.

Servants lined the steps to greet us. As our Rolls slowed to a halt, an attractive woman in her fifties royally descended the steps.

"My mother," whispered Cheng Shen.

I drew in my breath. Her clothes and bearing were impeccable. Climbing clumsily out of the car, I felt all the more like an elephant; my husband and I walked up to his mother who stood serenely at the base of the stairs.

"I am Mrs. Lam," she said.

"I am honored to be your daughter-in-law," I replied. "And this is your grandson, Chuin Man. He is two years old but slow to express himself."

"Good food and proper care can work miracles," she smiled.

"My daughter?" I asked. "How is she?"

"You will see her soon," she said. "Perhaps you should rest first, take a long leisurely bath."

As I bathed with scented soap in a marble tub, I couldn't believe it had only been days since I toiled on the coal mountain.

Then, once again, I gratefully held my daughter Chuin Way. How she had grown since our tearful good-byes in Canton months ago! She had become the darling of the Lam household. And when Ah Hsing related the harrowing details of their journey into Hong Kong, I could see even more clearly how the Lord was performing miracle after miracle in getting our family out of Red China.

We couldn't talk long; it was time for a special formality. It is a Chinese tradition for a new bride to serve tea to her husband's family at the wedding. Of course Cheng Shen's parents were in Hong Kong when we married, and it was now time for me to perform this ceremony. The immediate family sat down. I noticed Cheng Shen's father looked weak and pale, but I gave thanks he was well enough to be with us.

A tea service was ready; I poured tea in fine china cups and, bowing, handed them to my in-laws.

Then Mr. Lam clapped his hands, and a servant appeared carrying a silk-wrapped bundle. Cheng Shen's parents ceremoniously presented it to me. Within the silk were four gleaming bars of gold worth about twelve hundred Hong Kong dollars. With this gift I was officially received into the Lam family.

Later I went upstairs to our room where Cheng Shen was waiting. I stepped into it. The curtains were drawn diffusing the sunlight. The room was in shadows. At last we were alone. Cheng Shen stood at the window.

"Cheng Shen?"

He slowly turned, crossed the room. I held out my arms.

"You made it in your twenties after all," he said.

"When our son is born, I promise to be young again."

"Our son?"

"A boy for sure," I smiled shyly.

"You still think you know everything," he said quietly.

"No, just that I am delivering our second son to his father. He may walk out of this body at any moment." I pressed my face to his chest and murmured. "I have missed your presence."

Cheng Shen stepped back and turned to the window. I joined him and looked out on the modern skyline. "A city without red flags," I murmured.

I took his hand.

"My father refuses to die," said Cheng Shen.

"Thank God he is strong."

"He has many obligations. He is not charmed with a penniless son from China whose wife and children are refugees." Cheng Shen turned to me, his face concerned. "He has careful records, Neng Yee, of all the monies sent to us in Shanghai."

"But we are free now," I exclaimed. "We will work—pay back everything."

"But he does not expect to live that long," he cried. "The money from our safe deposit box will help. I must give it all to him to save our honor."

My hand flew to my mouth. "Cheng Shen, they would not let me take *anything* from China." I extended my empty ring finger. "Look, even our wedding ring had to remain behind. I came here with *nothing.*"

Cheng Shen stared at me for a moment, his jaw muscles working, then he drew back and slapped me.

I sank to the floor sobbing.

Cheng Shen slumped down on the floor next to me with tears in his eyes. "I am sorry, Neng Yee," he said. "You want to be first in line for everything. I want to go unnoticed . . . to be anonymous in the crowd." He looked away into the dark. "We are two friction points that can never find each other."

I reached up and took his arm. "The questions come as if we are still there. Then I check to see if my heart is dead."

However, I did not have much time to ponder Cheng Shen's feelings, for soon my labor pains began. An ambulance rushed me to the hospital. I was happy it was now going to be over, but frightened of what lay ahead.

In the hospital I lay in extreme pain. As a nurse wiped my face I pleaded, "Is something wrong? Tell me."

She shook her head. "The baby is very big. You must push."

I did. And the pains became insurmountable. "Oh, God!" I screamed, "help me!"

A few minutes later the nurse gently placed the crying baby besides me. "A fine son!" she soothed.

I touched his sleeping face. "Let me see you, oh 'child of the promise,' " I whispered.

I looked up at the nurse and thought of the coal pile, the long trip. "Is he well-formed?"

"Strong as a tiger," she smiled.

I was deliriously happy and thanked God for taking care of my baby. Yet, at the same time I had a foreboding of the future. There was Cheng Shen's strange actions. His concern about money. Only a week ago getting out of Red China had seemed the answer to all our troubles. Now, as I lay looking out the hospital window at a strange skyline, I wondered what lay ahead of us.

BELIEVING IN THE
IMPOSSIBLE

There was electricity in the air in the big stadium. I hung on the edge of my seat, thrilling to what was going on. But it wasn't a sports event. It was a church service, one like I had never seen before.

Not long after the birth of Chuin Mo, my "child of promise," I had started seeking a church. It was imperative I find one, especially with the strange way my husband was acting. And, as nice as Cheng Shen's parents were, I still felt a bit uncomfortable living in their house, impecunious as we were. And so with the memory of the house church in Shanghai fresh in my mind, I sought fellowship with kindred spirits.

But the churches I found did not have that spark, that excitement of feeling the presence of Jesus. Oh, they were pleasant enough with hymns sung, prayers read, and sermons spoken. The people were well dressed, the ushers polite. But they were not the same as that little Shanghai secret assembly who worshipped with such unashamed abandon.

Then I read about a series of meetings being held in Hong Kong's largest stadium; the article told about people being healed. And so on a cold December night in 1958 I ended up there.

The evangelist, who stood at the podium under hot stadium lights, was enthused: "Jesus can give us power to make us witnesses for Him to the world so that all men will come to know Him," he proclaimed. "He can heal our diseases, make the lame to walk, give hearing to the deaf, and speak directly to us."

I leaned forward, fascinated. "All these things can be yours today," he continued, "just as they were when Jesus walked the earth, because He still walks among us through His Holy Spirit!"

Then people went forward to receive Jesus as their Savior; others walked, limped, or were wheeled forward to receive healings. I watched a middle-aged woman swing herself up on crutches; two people placed their hands on her head, prayed for her, and she began to walk!

Night after night I went to the meetings fascinated by the healings. Yet I wondered about them. Back in China, a religious leader had told me that such healings happened only during the days of the early church. Yet here were people being healed today! I sought out a man who claimed he had been healed of a tumor.

"How do you know you've really been healed?" I asked.

He showed me a letter from his physician confirming it.

When I watched a woman rise from her wheelchair and walk, I approached her later and asked how long she had been confined to a wheelchair.

Her eyes shone as she exclaimed, "Praise God; for twenty years I was unable to take a step!"

I was impressed, but at the same time I was bothered. What about such healings being only for the time of the first disciples? When I brought this up to the evangelist, he replied; "Nowhere in the Bible does it say God put a time limit on healings. On the contrary, Jesus told His disciples they could do everything He did and *more*. And the Bible says all who follow Jesus today," he added meaningfully, "are His disciples."

Probably no one did more to convince me of the truth of this than the American evangelist, Kathryn Kuhlman, who appeared at one of the crusade meetings. When she first stepped onto the podium to speak, she made such a theatrical appearance in her flowing white dress that, frankly, I was turned off. But then when she began preaching, something electrifying happened. I *knew* the Holy Spirit was working through her and found myself enthralled. People all around me were being healed. A woman on my right stood up to say her pain from a slipped spinal disc was gone. A man behind me leaped up to announce his phlebitis had eased. And a little girl down in the front row who had a hearing problem told her mother she could understand Miss Kuhlman clearly!

Yes, I thought after the meeting was over, this woman was truly one of His disciples. I was sorry to see her return to the United States, not realizing that she would later become very important in my life. Soon the stadium meetings were over. To continue the ministry's work, a Christian Center was opened in downtown Hong Kong. During the crusade, I had volunteered to serve as an usher. Afterwards, the center's directors offered me work as a secretary and all-around helper. Because of our money problems, I was grateful and happily did everything from washing floors to scrubbing toilets.

With the extra money I earned, Cheng Shen did not complain about the time I spent at the Christian center. I thought how good everything seemed to be working out. But the most wonderful thing happened to me one Wednesday night at the close of a prayer meeting. The minister asked those who wanted to receive the Baptism of the Holy Spirit to come forward. I had read of this in the Bible, such as when the apostles received power from God in the Upper Room, and when Paul and the other apostles prayed for their followers to receive this anointing.

I wanted *everything* that Jesus had for me. So I went forward, kneeled, confessed my sins, yielded everything in my life to God, and asked Jesus to baptize me in His Holy Spirit.

An amazing and unexpected thing happened. All my fear and hatred of my persecutors in Red China, the Japanese who took our home, yes, even my poor old step-grandmother and mean cousins, left me. Instead I was overwhelmed with a new kind of love for everyone who had mistreated me. I knew I would never be the same again.

Of course, I still had a lot of growing to do. And one of my biggest stumbling blocks was money. When the minister preached, "The Lord loves a cheerful giver," I twisted uncomfortably in my pew. Well, I argued to myself, that is fine for people with money. But Cheng Shen was bringing in a very small salary. And I was making only one hundred and fifty dollars a month at the center. We couldn't afford to give anything. So when the offering basket came to me, I busied myself reading the Bible, or studied a tract.

One night in January I listened to missionaries talk of the desperate need for funds to pay bills for the stadium crusade and to continue the outreach program in Hong Kong.

"Lord, You surely understand why I can't give anything," I prayed. "If it weren't for Cheng Shen's parents, my family would be starving. I'm a refugee who brought nothing from China, not even my wedding ring."

But you have four bars of gold in the safe-deposit box here in Hong Kong.

I sat up startled. "Oh, but You don't understand, Lord," I pleaded. "Those gold bars are our emergency fund. If anything should happen to Cheng Shen or I can't work, we'll need them to feed the family."

He did not answer. But I felt no peace. Finally, I

decided to make a real sacrifice. I went to the bank, got two of the four gold bars and brought them to church. When the offering basket came, I proudly placed them in it. The usher almost dropped the basket, and I was pleased to see the startled look on his face. If he only knew, I thought, I had given God half of all that I owned in the world.

That night I couldn't sleep. I tossed and turned and in my heart I knew why. Finally, God spoke to me:

My daughter, haven't I proved to you time and time again that I am able to supply all your needs, even for things money can't buy? Don't you realize you don't need an emergency fund when you have Me?

I lay there staring into the darkness thinking of the miraculous ways in which He had provided for me all my life. My family's miraculous escape to Chungking, surviving the deadly persecution of the Communists, keeping my unborn child alive while I worked on coal mountain, and . . . most unforgettably, I heard the rifle's roar and felt nothing.

Could any amount of gold have paid for *that* protection?

"Oh Father," I cried, "forgive me, forgive me!"

The next morning found me standing outside the bank waiting for it to open. Inside I told the attendant: "You may refund my two dollars for the key to my safe-deposit box because I won't be needing it anymore."

That evening in church when the offering basket reached me, I placed my last two bars of gold in it. They were wrapped in cloth; I did not want to make a show of it. In God's eyes, I knew they were nothing. But in giving them, I felt I was finally giving Him myself entirely.

"I am Yours, Father, completely Yours." I prayed, "You are in charge of my life now. Do with me what You will."

Strange, unexpected things began to happen.

Mother, whom I left behind in Red China, was always

on my mind. I felt my brother Neng Yao would be safe for the time being. But Mother's father had been a wealthy merchant. Even more dangerous was the fact that she had been a childhood friend of the girl who later became Madame Chiang Kai Shek.

As the Communists had practically eliminated all the landowners, I knew they would begin combing the rest of the populace for "enemies of the state." And Mother would soon be under persecution. Her heart had been giving her more and more trouble lately, and I was fearful as to what she could stand.

Moreover, reports filtering from Red China revealed that the government's Great Leap Forward program was only a paper success. Chairman Mao's people, in their anxiety to build steel production and industry, had diverted millions of farmers from their land. As a result, food shortages had become even more severe, and my heart broke thinking my little mother faced possible starvation.

Yet, I could think of no way to persuade the authorities to give her an exit permit. The government was so capricious in these things. And I know they would dismiss any pleas from someone living in exile.

But I continued praying for her release.

Unbeknownst to me God had a plan.

On January 4, 1960, I accompanied our church youth group to a nearby fishing village where we ministered to the people who lived on sampans in the harbor. We had handed out literature, led several people to the Lord, and our group had assembled on the wharf getting ready to leave.

Someone accidentally bumped me and I fell twenty feet into the harbor. I awakened in the Queen Mary hospital with a shattered left ankle and a concussion. Church friends who had been praying for me said that, as the tide was out, I had fallen on large rocks protruding out of the shallow water.

When Cheng Shen came to the hospital, he looked

troubled: "I hate to tell you this, Neng Yee," he said, "but some of my relatives who do not believe as you do are snickering. 'How could a caring God,' they say, 'allow you to fall into that stinking harbor and nearly get killed when you were working for Him.' "

"I have no answer, my husband," I said, "All I know is that He has promised that all things will work out for good for those who love Him."

What really hurt was Ah Hsing, the nanny who brought my daughter Chuin Way to Hong Kong. She was a devout Buddhist, but I had been talking to her about the Lord, and she had seemed interested.

But now she had questions. "I cannot understand, Missy," she said, her eyes downcast, "how a real God could let such a terrible thing happen to you."

"I don't know, Ah Hsing," I said, "but I'm sure something good will come of it."

As I recuperated at home, God gave me two visions. One afternoon, as I lay alone in my bedroom I saw myself standing before thousands of blue-eyed, round-eyed black and white people talking about Jesus.

The other vision came one morning. As a breeze gently billowed the curtains, I heard God speak: *Neng Yee, the opportunity for your Mother to leave Red China is at hand.*

I was also given the strong feeling that *I* had to do something also. A pastor had once told me to pray as if everything depended on God, and to work as if everything depended on me. "Such work is your step of faith," he said.

I knew what my step of faith would be. With Ah Hsing's help, I took a taxi to the emergency room of the Queen Mary Hospital. There I got a written report of my accident along with copies of the X-rays. I sent them to my mother. "Submit all this to the authorities with your request for an exit permit," I wrote, "so you can come and help me with my babies during my convalescence."

For six weeks I waited for word. None came. Then it was time for my cast to be removed. New X-rays were taken and when the doctor examined them he shook his head. "I'm very sorry," he said, "but the bone was not set correctly. It must be rebroken and set again."

"Oh Lord, why?" I cried.

Have I forsaken you, my child, He said. Haven't I promised that all things work out for good?

"Yes, Lord," I wept, "but I can't see any good in having my ankle broken again and having to lie here for another six weeks of misery. And," I sniffled, "people are still laughing at me for my faith. What do You want me to do?"

Send medical reports on your new operation to your mother now.

The second operation took place in March and a fat bundle of certified documents went to Mother right afterwards.

The cast came off in May and I was able to walk on crutches. In the meantime, my pastor said the church had been praying daily for Mother's release.

But May passed, and most of the summer, with still no word from the mainland. Was my Mother even alive? I worried.

To make things worse, Cheng Shen was getting more and more irrational. His worry over money got the better of him, and he began physically abusing me, kicking and slapping me. I dared not tell anyone but the Lord.

One night when our church was in the midst of a revival, I arrived home about ten o'clock, too tired even to undress. I just threw myself across the couch and fell asleep.

I was awakened by a young woman in a shining robe standing in my room. I immediately thought of the old man who used to visit me and knew she was an angel.

"Neng Yee," she said. "The Lord has heard your

prayers and has a message for you. Your mother will be coming out of Red China tomorrow. Get everything ready."

I was so excited, even though it was three o'clock in the morning, I awakened my husband, the children, Ah Hsing, telling them what God had told me. Of course, everyone thought I was irrational.

"You are simply spending too much time at that church," snapped Cheng Shen.

My heart was too full to pay any heed to them. The next morning I arranged to rent a room for my mother. That night after the prayer meeting, I arrived home late in the evening. To my surprise everyone was still awake. *What was wrong?* I wondered.

Cheng Shen, who had an awed look, pointed to a telegram on the table.

It was from my mother.

"I am on my way to you, Neng Yee," it read.

The wire had been sent from Macao, only forty miles away. My mother had come out of Red China that very day, just as God had said she would!

As I read the wire aloud, I heard a crash from the kitchen. I rushed in to see Ah Hsing standing with tears in her eyes. At her feet were fragments of what had been a statue of Buddha.

"Oh, mistress," she cried. "I have served Buddha all my life. I didn't trust your Lord; I thought you had to be crazy to believe in what you couldn't see. But last night you told us what He promised and today a telegram comes saying it's true. I want to know your God. I want your Jesus to be my Jesus!"

She rushed into my arms.

The next day I went to Macao to get my mother who miraculously had no trouble getting across No Man's Land.

She explained what had happened to bring it about.

When my first medical report and X-rays arrived, she

thought they were something I made up in my desperation and did nothing, believing the Communists would laugh at it.

But when the second documents about my bone not being set properly came, *that* did it. With them she got her exit visa. It was now clear to me. Without my ankle being broken the second time, Mother would have never escaped Red China. Soon after she left, the flow of refugees was halted. There just wasn't space, food, or living accommodations in Hong Kong to accommodate the ever-increasing hordes of refugees.

Mother now realized a miracle had happened. Moreover, she couldn't get over the strength with which she was infused when it came time to make the trip. "I had no weakness at all, I felt like I could keep going forever. And your brother, Neng Yao, is well taken care of by relatives."

She wept. "I know it is because of your faith that I am here today, Neng Yee," she said. "Once I was not so sure, but now my faith is renewed."

As I put my arms around my little mother, my cup overflowed. But even then I would have not been able to believe His many miracles yet to come.

TO A FAR COUNTRY

For some reason I could not yet understand, God began putting me through a series of unbelievable situations.

The first involved my applying for a job as a social worker with the city of Hong Kong. After working at the Christian center for two years, I had become a school teacher of fifth-grade children, but my income was still inadequate. Cheng Shen, the children, and I had moved from his family's home into an apartment in a large building. And the rent was straining our budget.

Then I found a newspaper ad seeking applicants for a job as a social worker with the city of Hong Kong. I was excited and showed the ad to a friend.

"Wouldn't this be a wonderful way to help refugees like me and witness to them as well?" I exclaimed.

"You're dreaming, Neng Yee," she said. "Not only do they want people with perfect English for a job like that, but I understand the examinations are so tough only a few pass. They want people with real administrative abilities."

"Oh," I said, feeling crushed. But the more I thought about it, the more I believed if God wanted me to have that job, He would arrange it. Look what He had done for my mother.

I went to the office to fill out the application and when I learned the salary was 760 Hong Kong dollars a month, I was even more excited. But then the clerk said: "There will be two examinations, one written, one oral."

I turned away crestfallen again. How could I even begin to pass either one with my limited English? Then I brightened. "If I don't step into the Red Sea, it will never part," I said to myself.

For three days I haunted the main library studying books about Hong Kong, memorizing important details such as its population mix, civic problems, and the city's hopes for the future.

Even so, when I showed up for the tests and saw all the other applicants, I felt like slinking out the room. I knew many were graduates of Hong Kong University. They all looked so elegant and conversed in fluent English. What chance would I have?

Suddenly my name was called for the oral test.

The examiner sat behind a desk and asked me how long I had been in Hong Kong, my education, and other details. My tongue seemed stuck to the roof of my mouth, and I wasn't sure he understood my hesitant answers.

The written test was to take three hours, and we were not permitted to ask questions of the supervisors. But no one said I couldn't talk to God, so when I was handed the test papers, I prayed, "Lord, I understand that You spoke to the prophets and wrote the Bible through them. If You want me to work in social welfare, You are going to have to give me the words to write."

The first question asked: "Why do you want to work with the welfare department?" As a refugee whose heart felt for other refugees, that was an easy one. The second question involved a case study of a sampan family. Having met a number of these people the day I fell into the harbor, that, too, was simple.

After about fifty minutes, having written all that I could, I stood up from my desk to see everyone else writing furiously. Not thinking anymore about it, I handed in my test and went home.

A friend who had also taken the same test phoned me later that day. "You left so early, Neng Yee. Did you give up?" she asked. "No one else left before the three hours were up."

Well, I told myself, if God didn't want me to have that welfare job, then so be it.

A few weeks later I was called for a second interview by the chief of the Child Welfare Section of the Department.

I walked into the chief's office to find a sober looking woman studying me as I sat down. My heart was pounding. For a few moments she continued looking at me, her face impassive behind glasses glinting off the fluorescent ceiling lights.

Finally, she spoke. "It's strange," she said, "this normally doesn't happen to me, but I got a strong leading to interview you instead of the others."

My heart jumped, and then I relaxed. The interview completed, she rose from her desk and said, "You need to give us a character reference from your minister, and take a physical examination."

I stood up, confused.

"Yes," she smiled, "you have the job."

As I walked out of her office after thanking her, I noticed a small crucifix on the wall by her door.

"Thank You, Father," I whispered.

As a child welfare worker, I called on hundreds of destitute families on behalf of their children. It was a joy to be able to help them with food and clothing, and even more wonderful to tell them about Jesus, Who could meet all their needs.

And they really needed Him. For I began getting first-hand accounts of a growing horror in Red China called the Cultural Revolution. So-called Red Guards, really misguided youths, were let loose on the populace to persecute "class enemies." Killings and torture escalated.

I heard one terrible story of a Chinese pastor who was forced into a pine coffin and asked to deny his God. He wouldn't and they nailed the lid down. Still he wouldn't re-cant. Angrily, they lowered his coffin into the earth with the muffled voice of the pastor still heard praying as they shoveled dirt on it.

Hearing such stories made me want to help these refu-gees all the more. However, after several months Cheng Shen became even more irrational. Finally, I decided to stop work entirely and devote all my time to him. He might feel more secure, and we once again could be a happy family, I hoped.

It didn't work.

The first week after I resigned, Mother became ill and I called a doctor. Later that day Cheng Shen came home complaining he lost a hundred dollars from his pocket. When he heard about the doctor, he accused me of stealing his money to pay the physician. He flew into a rage, slapping and kicking me.

For the first time, I told Cheng Shen's mother how her son was mistreating me, hoping she might be able to help him. But she refused to believe me. His cruelty increased, and one day I became so despondent I found myself on the roof of our thirteen-story apartment building.

I leaned on the waist-high parapet staring sadly down to the street far below. People looked like ants and sounds of traffic drifted faintly up. I thought how simple it would be to escape all the misery. At this height, death would be quick and easy. Lost in agony, I started to climb onto the narrow ledge when I felt a tugging at my shoe and a frightened little voice calling, "Mama, Mama, I need you."

I turned to see little Chuin Man standing there looking up at me, tears running down his face. He had followed me up the stairs to the roof. I fell from the parapet back onto the graveled rooftop and lay there weeping, while my son squatted beside me, patting my hair to comfort me.

Restored to reality, I asked God to forgive me, realizing that my life didn't belong to me. It belonged to Him. And He had work for me to do, besides caring for my mother and children.

Still, I couldn't understand why my husband who had seemed to love me so much had turned so against me. In prayer and opening myself to the Holy Spirit I sought an answer. I believe it was given to me. Cheng Shen's sad childhood had left an indelible impression on him. I felt the many lonely months he had suffered from tuberculosis when he believed he wouldn't live long had much to do with his morosity and his changeable moods. Moreover, his father had many concubines and, as a result, Cheng Shen found himself just one of many brothers and sisters. So many, perhaps, that he never felt part of a close-knit family with strong ties that would sustain him later in life. Thus I felt that Cheng Shen was never really himself when he struck me.

My pastor, Rev. Bill Thornton, who couldn't help notice the bruises on my arm, the black eye, the burn on my leg, suspected where they came from. It broke my heart to admit he was right. He felt that for my and the children's safety, I should live apart from my husband.

However, Cheng Shen was drinking heavily at the time, and I felt if I left him he would kill me. What could I do? I lay awake at night trembling, praying for guidance.

It came in a letter from Kathryn Kuhlman.

She wrote that she had heard how I had been telling others how I had escaped from Red China, about my struggle in giving the four bars of gold to the missionaries, and other lessons learned. She wanted me to come to the United States to speak at her gatherings. If I were interested, an airline ticket and expenses would be forthcoming.

Were those visions God had given me about speaking before blue-eyed, round-eyed black and white people going to come true? I wondered.

It was beyond anything I could imagine. In all the nine years I had been living in Hong Kong, I had never spoken before a large group of people. I did a lot of praying for guidance; God seemed to say "Go." Mother said she'd be happy to take care of the children while I was gone. Cheng Shen was moody about it but realized under the circumstances he couldn't forbid me.

When I said good-bye to Mother she said, "People in the United States will have a difficult time with your name, Neng Yee, so I will give you an American name to use. From now on you will be 'Nora.' " I liked the sound of it and kissed her. "Thank you, Mother, for such a nice going-away gift."

When the plane roared off the runway over the South China Sea, I looked back at the city where my loved ones lived and wondered if I was doing the right thing. I had a lot of time to think on that long flight and whenever I had qualms about leaving home, the Lord always sustained me.

You have work to do, Neng Yee.

We landed in Los Angeles and one of Miss Kuhlman's people was there to meet me. She said that a local minister who had met me in Hong Kong asked if I could speak at his church before going on to Miss Kuhlman's headquarters.

I agreed and was driven to his church. On the way I was amazed by the number of automobiles, the superhighways, the many tall buildings. I had heard many stories about America but never expected anything like *this*. I was overwhelmed.

When it came time for me to speak at the church, I looked around for the interpreter. There was none. I would have to speak in English. I panicked.

"Lord, what am I going to do?"

It's not what you are going to do, He answered, *it's what I am going to do through you. Just yield yourself to Me.*

I stepped up into the pulpit, my knees shaking and poured out what was in my heart. I don't know if they understood a word of what I said. But I knew God had done something in spite of my inadequacy.

Then I was whisked to Pittsburgh where I boarded a bus to go to Miss Kuhlman's big meeting in Youngstown, Ohio. Buses filled with hundreds of people seemed to be going to the same place, and I wondered what I was getting into.

When we arrived, the big auditorium was jammed with eight thousand people. Miss Kuhlman asked me to come to the microphone and tell my life story.

I was so nervous I couldn't speak. So Miss Kuhlman started off asking me what I liked best about America so far.

"McDonald's hamburgers and Kentucky Fried Chicken," I blurted.

The crowd roared in laughter, and suddenly I felt among friends. Looking out on all those smiling faces, I spoke from my heart.

"Just before he died, my father told me to come to you blue-eyed, round-eyed black and white people, and I have finally found you. Your American missionaries told me about Jesus, so we are not strangers. I'm your sister, and you are my brothers and sisters." I broke down. Recovering, I continued, "I never cried in front of my enemy, but I am crying in front of you, because you will love me and you will remember my tears and my people in your hearts."

Miss Kuhlman said, "Yes, honey, we are your American family!" And all eight thousand people rose to their feet and applauded. When they finally sat down, I went on talking to them from the bottom of my heart. It took nearly two hours to tell them all God had done for me, and when I finished, Miss Kuhlman stood up, cried, and put her arm around me.

"The calling of God is on you, beloved," she said. "Your story should be told all over the world."

For weeks I traveled with Miss Kuhlman. She taught me American office procedures, introduced me to all her friends in restaurants and department stores, even to the policemen who handled the traffic at her meetings. I told the story about the four gold bars many times.

After a month and a half traveling with Miss Kuhlman the Lord made it clear to me that it was time for me to move on. *I haven't brought you here to be part of Miss Kuhlman's ministry forever,* He said, *I have prepared you for a ministry of your own.*

It was difficult to leave Miss Kuhlman. But when a San Diego woman who had heard my testimony when I first landed in America invited me to her home I took it as God's will.

One night at dinner she told me an amazing story.

"You know, Nora, when you spoke that first night, many people complained that you talked so rapidly and with such poor English they couldn't understand a word you said."

I stopped eating and stared at her. I knew I was a poor speaker but was my English *that* bad?

She put her hand on my arm and continued. "Furthermore, you sounded so bitterly anti-Communist that you almost made them sympathize with your enemies!

"But do you know what happened? One of the most despicable men in town, a man who had never set foot in a church before, had come to the meeting out of curiosity to hear a Chinese woman tell how she escaped from Communist China."

"I suppose he had a good laugh," I said glumly, looking into my tea cup.

"No," she said, "on the contrary. Something you said

touched him so that two weeks later he came back to church to give his life to God."

I stared at her; then it might be true after all. God *did* have a ministry for me in America.

Encouraged as I was, I was so lonesome for my children that I couldn't stand it. In September of 1966, I decided to return to Hong Kong to bring them and Cheng Shen back to the United States with me. I hoped that America was so far from all his memories of Communist persecution that Cheng Shen would get hold of himself and become a loving husband again.

Again, I had to say good-bye to Mother, promising to bring her to the United States when it was possible. The children, Cheng Shen, and I flew to America to start a new life in Hayward, California.

The Alcoholics Anonymous people call what I tried to do for Cheng Shen a "geographical cure," and they are right in saying it never works. For Cheng Shen brought all his problems to the United States with him. He continued abusing and threatening to kill me.

A lawyer advised me that if I did not leave my husband at once, my children would soon be without a mother. And when I prayed, I was given confirmation that it was right to escape.

Leaving Cheng Shen was the most difficult thing for me to do, but for my children's sake I had to do it. One day in February 1967, I took the children out of school in Hayward and we went to the airport to take a plane to Denver. An American couple I had met in Hong Kong some years earlier lived in Denver and offered us a place to stay until we knew what we would finally do.

As we sat in the airport waiting for the boarding announcement, my heart cried out for the children. It seemed all my life I had been a refugee, from a child escaping to

Chungking, a pregnant mother fleeing to Hong Kong, and now my three children were refugees also.

I looked at them obediently waiting.

By this time they all bore American names which a missionary friend had suggested. "It will help them fit in better," she suggested. She was right; they had already made good friends in school, and now I felt terrible relocating them to where they would have to develop new relationships all over again. But it was for their good, I kept telling myself.

As I watched them, my heart filled. Eleven-year-old Paul (Chuin Man) was reading a book, ten-year-old Ruth (Chuin Way) was talking to her doll, and eight-and-a-half-year-old Joseph (Chuin Mo) was coloring a picture.

Our flight was called; the three of them carefully put their things away and joined me. I was so proud of them as we walked to the plane. Again, I thought how God uses everything for good. Cheng Shen's and my relationship had not worked out, but from it came these three beautiful children.

While we lived in Denver, my lawyer notified me that my husband had refused to contribute to the support of our children and I did something that I didn't think I would ever consider. I went to Las Vegas to establish residence so I could file for divorce. When the proceedings were finally settled, I was awarded full custody of the children.

However, as a divorced woman, I believed no one would ever want me to speak in their pulpit. So I thought I would go back to law school to earn a degree that would be recognized in the United States.

But providing for my children took precedence over my personal plans. And I stayed in Las Vegas for several years working at whatever job I could find, as a cook preparing Chinese cuisine for the Stardust Hotel, an accountant, a public-school teacher's aide, a grocery-store clerk. I even worked in a bank, unlocking a door to let people go to their safe-deposit boxes. Everytime I helped someone, I couldn't help but think of the last time I went to my own safety-deposit box to get out those last two bars of gold. I never regretted it.

For it was true; when you give yourself entirely to God, you make the way open for Him to work miracles in your life.

One night I received a phone call.

"Nora Lam? I'm a pastor in California and a friend who heard you speak a few years ago told us about you. Our people would like to hear your story," he said, "would you come and speak to us?"

Of course, I was happy to do so. This was the beginning of many similar invitations. Sometimes, I found myself speaking four times on a single day on a weekend.

I didn't really enjoy telling my story, and I would cry as I again lived through all the pain and heartache. But the listeners seemed moved, and I felt America needed to be warned of the dangers of Communism before it was too late.

Soon I was away every weekend. And again, good things came from a seemingly impossible situation. I wired my mother to come to live with me and help take care of the children.

She was delighted, and when I met her at the airport, I couldn't help but think of God's promise that my whole family would be out of Red China one day. I felt sure my brother would make it eventually. Then my heart caught when I thought about father in his grave in Shanghai. He never did leave Red China. But later, I learned God had His own ideas on this situation, also.

With Mother on hand to help, I was free to speak for my Lord. And for five years I traveled from city to city telling my story. Then God asked me to do the impossible.

BACK TO THE
DRAGON

I was aghast at what I was being told.

It happened one evening in 1971 in Las Vegas while resting from my day working as a teacher's aide. Though weekends found me flying to various churches to tell my story, life had begun to settle down. The children were happy in school, and my mother was helping make our home a pleasant retreat.

She was sitting across the room from me embroidering, and I had been reading the Bible. I placed it on my lap to rest my eyes when His Word came.

Nora, I want you to go to Taiwan, the free Republic of China, to preach to my people there.

Taiwan?

I must have flinched noticeably. For Mother looked up from her embroidery. "Neng Yee," she exclaimed, "what's wrong?"

"Nothing, Mother," I replied, "just nerves, I guess."

I couldn't bring myself to reveal this unbelievable directive. I well remembered vowing never to return to Taiwan after my aborted stay many years ago. Moreover, it was much too close to Red China. I could almost feel the breath of that angry dragon.

"Lord," I begged, "please do not ask me to go back to China."

Nora, I didn't bring you here to preach only to the Americans. I brought you here to learn what you would need to know to minister to your own people.

"But Father, I'm afraid to go. I don't have a single friend in Taiwan. Besides, nobody there would ask a woman preacher to speak."

The thought was so outrageous that I wondered if I had imagined the Lord's directive. So I forgot about it. A week later our phone rang.

"Nora Lam?" It was a male voice.

"Yes?"

"This is Jim Gerrard. I'm with the Full Gospel Businessmen's Fellowship, and I believe I have a special message for you. Would it be all right to come by and see you next Saturday afternoon?"

The meeting seemed so important to him that I said yes.

Then I checked with some Christian friends to see if they had ever heard of him. "Oh yes," one remarked. "He's well-known. You might call him a modern-day prophet. When the Lord tells him that a thing will happen, it always happens."

So I was quite curious as I waited to meet him in the Las Vegas airport that Saturday. When this tall, thin man walked up the runway, I was struck by his other-worldly appearance.

"God has a message for you, Nora Lam," he said on greeting me. Later in my living room he told me what prompted him to call me. He had never heard of me until recently when attending a Full Gospel meeting. There someone mentioned my name; he knew immediately that the Lord had a message for me, and he was supposed to deliver it.

Everything within me rebelled at what he was about to say, but I knew I had to listen.

"Nora Lam," he said, "the Lord has told me that He created you to bear this message—that you would be a vessel to reach all of China for Jesus. First, He is going to use you to reach the people of Taiwan with the message of the gospel. He will communicate to them from the top to the bottom—all the way from the leaders in the palaces down to the most humble barefoot peasant working in the rice paddies."

I stared at him, my heart pounding.

"And when revival has begun in Taiwan," he continued, "the door of Red China will be open to you. You will go in to minister to your Chinese people—one-fifth of the world's population. You will win them for Jesus. He will use Taiwan as the door to break through to the whole country of Red China."

He finished the prophecy, ending with "Thus saith the Lord."

I shook my head in disbelief. Surely, this man was out of his mind. I thanked him politely, we had dinner, and I saw him off on a late evening flight.

But all the while my mind was racing. How wrong could someone be? I was no Billy Graham, and Red China would never be open to me. I remembered the Shanghai police officer who had thrown my exit permit at me thirteen years ago and shouted at me to stay out of Red China forever.

Even so, the logic of the prophecy would not elude me. All that night as I relived those words I knew in my heart that Taiwan and mainland China would *have* to be won for the Lord by Chinese people. I knew that sainted missionaries had introduced the gospel to China and many had given their lives to do so. But it would take Chinese evangelists to reach the masses there.

Americans and other Western people are totally different from the Chinese in culture, speech, in ways of thinking. And even though Westerners may be fluent in Chinese, they still can't speak "the same language."

I had already seen this in the United States. Americans are so openly expressive; they tell you what they think. But the Chinese are reserved. Even if there is a problem, they'll bow and smile, pretending everything is all right.

As I considered these facts, all my arguments against going to Taiwan began to shrivel. Yes, God could use me there, I finally believed. But He would have to make the way possible. As for Red China, that was too preposterous even to consider.

Even so, I dragged my feet about going. It was the children that held me back. I didn't want to go halfway around the world. I wanted to be home with Ruthie, Paul, and Joe, to tuck them into bed, hear their prayers.

One afternoon the phone rang. "Mrs. Lam, I'm calling from the hospital emergency room. I'm afraid there's been an accident. . . ."

It was Ruth. A car in which she had been riding was struck by another automobile. She had been brought to the hospital unconscious. They didn't know the full extent of her injuries.

Cold fear gripped me as I rushed to the hospital. For three hours I waited, praying, weeping. Finally a nurse came out and told me that Ruth had regained consciousness. There were no broken bones. And when she was brought out to me, other than bits of glass in her hair and a torn sweater, she didn't have a scratch.

I thanked God all through the night for saving Ruth. I also did not miss the lesson. My staying in Las Vegas to be near my children did not in any way protect her from having an accident. But the Lord was there. No matter where I traveled in the world, He would be *there* with them.

Within a few days I was on a plane bound for Taiwan. I had absolutely no idea of what I would do when I arrived, except the certainty that God had plans.

Many long hours later I landed in the capital city of Taipei. It was so different from the city I had visited many years ago. Now it was a modern metropolis with skyscrapers and streets filled with cars, buzzing motorbikes, and bicycles.

"Where do you want me to preach, Father?" I prayed. He had other ideas.

One of mother's friends who lived in Taiwan phoned me at the hotel on my arrival. I'm sure my mother let her know I was arriving.

"I know you are a friend of Kathryn Kuhlman and you believe in divine healing," she said.

She went on to explain that a high-ranking military leader, General Wu Sung Ching, had been critically injured in an auto accident. He was in a hospital in Kaohsiung, another city. Could I go up there to pray for him? She said the general's friends, whom she knew quite well, told her they expected him to die anyway, so my praying for him would do no harm.

"Well, Lord," I sighed, "instead of speaking to a crowd of people, you want me to start with one man? All right, I will go."

But when I stepped into the general's hospital room, I almost wished I hadn't come. Unconscious, and almost hidden in surgical dressings, he had suffered broken bones, severe lacerations, and multiple bruises. Moreover, the grim-looking armed guards at his bedside made me very uncomfortable.

If I pray, I worried, and God doesn't raise him up, I could be in serious trouble. But then gaining confidence in knowing that I had come in the power of Jesus, I told the guards: "I want all of you to leave the room so I can pray."

"Why?" One argued, his eyes full of suspicion.

"Because you do not believe," I answered. "I cannot let you remain here and hinder my prayer."

They didn't move.

"If you don't leave, I won't pray."

They filed out of the room, and I opened my Bible. After reading a few verses out loud, I spoke to the general. Though he was not conscious, I knew his spirit could hear me. "The doctors say you were very seriously injured, General Wu. But our God is real and I say you're going to be healed. I'm going to pray for you now. I *know* He can raise you up."

Then I laid my hands on his quiet form, praying: "In the name of Jesus Christ, be healed . . ."

I saw nothing happen but I wasn't discouraged. I had done my part. The healing was up to God.

After interceding for General Wu, I faced the problem of finding a pastor who would let me in his pulpit. My situation looked impossible.

"With what ministry are you affiliated," demanded the first one I approached, "Billy Graham, Oral Roberts?"

"I belong to Jesus," I answered. "I'm here because He has sent me."

Every door slammed. I was wondering if I would have to preach on street corners when I remembered the Reverend Matthew Lee, a Taipei pastor whose church Kathryn Kuhlman had helped build.

"In China, we don't have women evangelists," he snapped. "Besides, you're not officially associated with Kathryn Kuhlman, and we've never heard of you," he said, adding: "My deacons wouldn't like it if I invited a woman to preach."

"Please pray about it," I said, "if the Lord doesn't want you to open the door, all right. But if He wants you to open it. . . ."

He agreed to pray for three nights.

Four days later he called me to say he had scheduled me to speak for six nights of revival, from Tuesday through Easter Sunday night.

Only fifty people came Tuesday night. Shaking with nervousness, I poured out my life story. It was the first time I had opened my heart to a congregation of my own people. The next night attendance was a little larger. But before I had a chance to speak, one member of the congregation stood up.

"My name is C.P. Ying," he announced. "When I came to this service last night, I had been blind in one eye for many years. As I listened to Nora Lam, I felt the power of God touch me. Today I can see! My doctor has confirmed that my eye is healed of blindness. Praise God, I can *see!*"

The others sat there stunned.

Word of the miracle spread like a string of exploding firecrackers, and by Thursday night the little church was jammed with six hundred people. Many gave their hearts to the Lord, and He healed many people.

Then God ordered me to do something I thought ridiculous.

Close the meeting.

"It doesn't make sense, Lord," I argued.

You must make room for Me to move. He directed. *I want you to rent the largest indoor stadium in the city for Saturday night and Sunday.*

When I announced this to the congregation, everyone including the pastor was as dumbfounded as I.

The next morning I stood on the sidewalk in front of the largest indoor stadium in Taipei. It could seat eighteen thousand people. I was frightened. I had no board of deacons, no sponsor, no advance team to set things up. Everybody would know I was mad if I scheduled a meeting in such a mammoth place with only one day's notice. Experienced evangelistic teams usually take a year to plan such a meeting.

Right, Nora. No man can do it. But I can do it. If you will obey Me, I will save souls, heal the sick, give sight to the blind, open deaf ears, heal wounded hearts . . .

I still thought it was impossible.

You do the possible, He said gently, *and I'll take care of the impossible.*

Standing in front of the stadium, I took a deep breath, closed my eyes and said, "In the name of Jesus, I claim this stadium for Your revival."

When I opened my eyes, I saw a puzzled-looking man standing in front of me. "What on earth are you doing here?" he asked.

"I have just claimed this stadium for the Lord to use tomorrow night and Sunday," I answered.

He laughed. "You'd better forget it because I'm the manager and I know the stadium has been rented for a national ballgame to be held this week."

He started to turn away when I said, "Using the stadium wasn't my idea, it was God's." He turned back with a surprised look and I added: "Frankly, I'd rather be home with my children for Easter. But God is in charge and you had better let Him use it."

He shook his head, laughed again, and said, "Okay, okay, just to make you and God feel better, excuse me while I'll phone the owner and confirm the fact it's rented."

He returned with a stupefied look. I don't know what was said on the telephone. Maybe the game had been cancelled, or the ballplayers had transportation problems. But we could have the stadium!

"Now the important question," he said. "Can you afford it?"

I looked straight at him. "My Father is so rich that He owns all the cattle on a thousand hills."

"Oh," he seemed impressed, "he's a wealthy rancher?"

"Much richer than a thousand ranchers," I replied.

"Well, come into the office," he said, "and we'll sign a contract."

His reaction gave me the courage to buy radio and

television time and a large newspaper ad to announce the meeting. I just signed and signed for all the publicity.

The miracle was that I didn't have to put any money down, something normally expected. Of course, I knew everyone would be paid. A good friend back in the United States had promised to cover expenses. He was S. K. Sung, whom I had met in Hong Kong where he had helped found a church. A man of God, he had dedicated himself to the Lord's work. After immigrating to the United States, he had encouraged my ministry among the Chinese people. However, if I had to take time beforehand to contact him for the money for the stadium and media announcements, none of it would have happened on schedule.

As it was, our stadium crusade opened the next night. The newspaper and broadcast advertising had done their work, and the place was packed.

I stood at the podium trembling as I looked out over the huge crowd of expectant people. Some sat in wheelchairs, others were blind, many were obviously ill.

Suddenly, I became terrified. I felt so insignificant. No one knew me. What right had I to stand up here and promise them something? And then of course, I knew, it wasn't in my strength I was here. It was in the power of Jesus.

After I began to speak, people whom God had restored, rushed forward. Some pushed wheelchairs they didn't need anymore, others had been healed of eye and ear problems. Later, over one hundred healings of cancer were verified by the hospital in Taipei.

By Easter Sunday night, more than six thousand people had streamed forward to accept the Lord.

I had learned a most important lesson from that Crusade. When God directs you to move, *move*. Don't wait for a "more advantageous" time. Step out in faith. Don't let Satan persuade you; it won't work. It *will* work—if you trust Him.

There was even a healing for me. As I was laying

hands on people at the last meeting, the surging crowd accidentally knocked me off the platform. Men helped me to my feet but I couldn't walk. My ankle had already begun to swell. Examination at the hospital revealed torn tendons, and doctors said it would be weeks before I would walk without pain.

To go home in a wheelchair just didn't seem right after all the Lord had done. Wanting all the prayers I could get, I telephoned my family and also S. K. Sung, my good Christian friend.

"Nora, I knew it already," said S. K. "At the same time you fell, I had been praying and saw a vision in which hundreds of devils were attacking you. I prayed mightily in the name of Jesus for your deliverance and saw the demons depart."

I felt better already. The next morning someone knocked on my hotel-room door. It was a woman friend whom I greeted enthusiastically.

"Would you pray for me?" I asked.

She placed her hands on my ankle and said, "Lord, You sent Nora here to do Your work. It isn't right for her to go home in a wheelchair. Please touch her ankle with Your perfect wholeness. In the name of Jesus, I pray. Amen."

At her simple prayer, every trace of pain left me, and I was able to rise and walk freely.

There was another healing in Taiwan during my visit. A week after I had prayed for General Wu Sung Ching in Kaohsiung, thanks be to God, he was released from the hospital, entirely well.

20

GOD'S CHAIN REACTION

Late in 1971 I faced one of the most crucial decisions of my life. Should I remain single or remarry?

S.K. Sung was the Christian man who had encouraged my ministry among the Chinese by paying all the expenses of my meetings in Taiwan. This tall handsome gentleman of quiet demeanor was a student of both Christianity and Chinese history. His family lineage went back thousands of years. And we shared the same abiding faith.

Yet, if I married, I knew I would be criticized by many people. But it wasn't man's approval I sought, it was God's will. What would *He* want me to do? So on December 2, 1971, I began to fast and pray seeking guidance. Days and weeks went by and I ate very little.

"Mother, your dress is hanging so loose on you, I'm worried," my daughter, Ruth, approached me in concern, for in a period of only weeks I had lost thirty pounds. Even the Christmas holidays could not affect my fast. For I found that, as Jesus taught, it is only through serious fasting and praying one can best discern God's leading. The more I fasted, the more I felt God wanted me to marry this special man. Yet, I prayed for some sign so I could be absolutely certain.

Any doubts were resolved one evening when I was alone in my bedroom. I had been deep in prayer and something caused me to look up. I gasped in surprise. It was the old man of my childhood, the very same white-bearded one who had visited me in my deep loneliness at my step-grandmother's house.

He wore the same long blue servant's overshirt, and his seamed face glowed with love. He smiled and nodded . . . and let me know it was definitely God's will. And so in January, 1972, I became Nora Lam Sung to the glory of God.

But there was little time for relaxation. God was already calling me back to Taiwan. Again I was reluctant to go, and again I sought confirmation.

As before, it came in unexpected ways.

One Sunday morning I was visiting an Assembly of God church in San Jose, California. After preaching on finding God's will, the pastor asked all who had ever made a commitment to God to step forward. Then he completely surprised me.

"And I want Nora Lam to lead the way," he said.

Trembling, I went forward and sank to my knees at the altar to pray with the others. Suddenly, I heard a woman beside me praying in perfect Mandarin, my native dialect.

"Sung Neng Yee," came the words, "I am coming soon. If you want to do something for Me, you've got to do it right now. I am calling you to Kaohsiung, Tainan, Hualein, and Taitung. . . ."

Shocked, I opened my eyes to see that the woman was Sue Westbrook, an American I had met several years before. I knew she couldn't speak a word of Chinese!

We both stared at each other, then fell into each other's arms crying. The pastor excitedly brought out a map of

Taiwan and put pins in the places that had been named in the prayer.

Similar confirmations happened again and again. Americans who could not speak Chinese, yet speaking under the power of the Holy Spirit, named the same cities.

Letters confirming God's calling came from overseas, the most persuasive one from General Wu who wanted ". . . to testify to the whole island of Taiwan that the Living God is a God of miracles."

We scheduled the crusades of October 1972.

But where would we get the money? My husband, S.K., had paid for the 1971 meetings in the Taipei stadium, but I couldn't expect one man to underwrite the expenses of four cities—sixteen days.

So people could at least begin setting up the crusades, I was able to borrow a thousand dollars from a relative and send it to Taiwan. Then two people sent in checks for five hundred dollars each. Well, that was another thousand.

But then came a directive from the Lord I could not understand. I met with a Reverend Bernard Johnson who was soon to return to mission work in Brazil. After we had prayed for each other, God asked me to give the thousand dollars to Reverend Johnson.

I couldn't understand it, nor did I want to do it, we were so desperate for funds in Taiwan. But I had no peace about it and finally surrendered.

I picked up the phone and called Bernard Johnson. "The Lord told me to give you a thousand dollars," I said. The phone was silent for a long moment, then sobs sounded over the wires; Bernard Johnson was crying. When he recovered, he said, "Do you know what, Nora Lam? The Lord had asked me to raise forty thousand for the work in South America. This is the last thousand I needed before my departure."

It was as if that difficult bit of obedience opened the

floodgates. Events happened in amazingly strange ways, each having an effect on the other.

The first took place when I had to decide between two invitations to speak, both on the same day. One was before a large meeting of nine thousand people. The other was at a little church in Sparks, Nevada. The Lord directed me to Sparks. Despite my misgivings, I went.

I questioned His guidance even more as I stood in the pulpit in Sparks. Only fifty people sat in the pews. "Lord," I breathed silently, "I need thirty-five thousand dollars and You bring me to a congregation with only fifty people?"

Just preach My Word.

I did, and when the pastor brought me to the airport, he handed me a check for $1,144.48.

"It's a miracle," he said with awe.

I was so thrilled that when I got home, I called one of our staff in Taiwan. "The Lord said great things would happen, and they've started," I enthused. "A little church with only fifty people sacrificed to give more than a thousand dollars!"

When I arrived in Taiwan, I walked into a gloomy meeting where ministers of six different denominations had gathered to plan the crusade.

They had been at an impasse, unable to agree on who would sit where on the platform and what forms of worship to follow.

"Oh, my brothers," I cried, "it is time for us to stop criticizing one another and work together. Just think: Fifty Americans in a tiny church in Nevada have emptied their pockets to help bring the gospel of salvation to our Chinese people!"

Visibly moved, the ministers looked at each other with new eyes, and a spirit of cooperation bloomed. They decided to cooperate in chartering buses to bring people to the crusade. They had a vision of tens of thousands flooding the stadiums, of healings and lives being changed. Enthused, they vowed to do everything to work together, all because of fifty generous Christians in Sparks, Nevada.

Miracles like this happened again and again, and in the hot summer of 1972 I flew back to Taiwan for sixteen nights of revival. I found the island alive with the Holy Spirit. It was the first time in history that 150 different churches had cooperated to sponsor a healing and evangelistic campaign.

In Kaohsiung, thousands who had already heard about General Wu, had walked for miles to hear him tell of his healing. They waited from four o'clock in the afternoon until ten in the evening so they could respond to an altar call.

Record-breaking crowds thronged the stadiums everywhere. In one city, the chief of police, a lifelong Buddhist with a tough reputation, came forward humbly to accept the Lord.

The forty-year-old daughter of the commander-in-chief of the armed forces in eastern Taiwan was healed of deafness in one ear. And then I'll never forget the teenage girl coming to the platform carrying on her back her aged mother who appeared to be blind and suffering from leprosy. She looked so terrible, I shrank back and all I could do was say the words "In the name of Jesus, be healed." The next day a smiling woman walked up holding the teenager's hand. Her skin was clear, her eyes open. "I am the woman you dared not touch, but I thank you for praying." She smiled. "Jesus has healed me."

People from all walks of life came to be healed, aged ones stricken with diseases, youths suffering from emotional problems. In one short month in 1972, twenty-two thousand people came forward to pledge their souls to Jesus.

During that crusade, I was glad for the opportunity to visit an old friend, Johnson Han, the director of the Bethany Children's Home in Taipei. Since I first met him the previous year, he and his children had become very dear to me.

Back then I asked what they wanted Jesus to do for them. One sober-faced little boy spoke up for the group and said, "It's so hot here in the summer we would like a swimming pool."

I was surprised. But all the children jumped up and down shouting: "Yes, a swimming pool! A swimming pool!"

When they finally quieted down, one little girl asked solemnly: "Could Jesus really give us something as big as that?"

"Of course, He can," I assured her, wishing I really believed it myself. "If you need a swimming pool, and you really and truly believe Jesus, He will get one for you."

Back then I was such a beginner in trusting the Lord for financial needs, I did have some doubts. But I didn't want the children to be disappointed.

When I returned to the United States, I began telling congregations across the land about the orphans who needed a swimming pool. But my English was still so poor that people probably didn't understand what I was talking about. And after several weeks, I had received only a little over three hundred dollars toward the pool. I was discouraged. Finally, the Lord spoke to me.

Neng Yee. You have a diamond ring now worth six thousand dollars. I want you to give it to help buy the swimming pool for the Bethany Children's Home.

"Lord," I argued, "I have only one ring, an engagement ring from S.K."

I know, that's why I want you to give it. I had only one Son.

When I sent the ring to Taiwan, people heard about it. And all at once they began to open their hearts and pocketbooks. They donated architectural services, cement, labor, and everything needed to build a beautiful Olympic-sized pool for the children.

At the time many criticized me for it. "So many children starving and you waste money on a swimming pool?"

But I knew God must have some reason for it. I wasn't to know that reason for seven years.

Obedience was a lesson I was beginning to learn. And each year the Lord ordered me back to Taiwan, I found it easier to go. But in 1973, while sitting in my Taipei hotel room, I couldn't believe what He was asking me to do.

I want you to go on radio and broadcast the gospel throughout Taiwan and even into Red China where people can listen by shortwave radio.

"But Lord, I'm no radio personality. I don't even know how to operate the machine."

You don't need to know how to operate anything. Just preach My Word.

"But I have the worst voice in the whole world. I'm a Pentecostal evangelist, and the people will turn me off the minute they hear me."

Don't worry about your voice, Nora. Your heart will speak.

"But Lord, it will cost too much . . ."

He answered my last argument with a telephone call. I was sitting in my room wondering how to arrange something with which I absolutely had no experience when the phone rang.

"Nora Lam, this is Lee Shih-feng, corporation president of the Broadcasting Company of China. Could we get together soon?"

Within an hour we were sitting together in the hotel coffee shop. As we became acquainted I learned his father had been a Methodist minister.

I was curious about what he wanted to talk about and couldn't get over the fact that here was one of the biggest men in Chinese radio sitting across the table from me just after God asked me to utilize this medium.

Then he told me why he called me: "I attended one of your evangelistic meetings last year in the sports stadium here," he said. "I was quite impressed and wanted to meet you."

"I didn't have anything to do with those healings, of course," I said. "You know they all came from the power of God."

He started to speak but I couldn't contain myself any longer and broke in. "The Lord wants me to begin radio broadcasting," I blurted. "If you could sell me time on your stations . . ."

He leaned back in the coffee-shop booth and smiled. "I'll be glad to let you have time on ten stations," he said, "and I can let you have it for only one hundred dollars a day."

I stared at him flabbergasted. This was more than I even hoped for.

He took out his pen, scribbled some figures on a napkin and pushed it at me. "You'll be able to reach seventeen million people in Taiwan, and hundreds of millions more in Mainland China."

"Please give me a contract before you change your mind!" I laughed.

Later, Mr. Lee increased the number of stations to nineteen without any additional charge. God had provided . . . and quickly, too.

I started making tapes for broadcasting over the stations back in my home in America. My original sound room was a walk-in closet with an old-fashioned reel-to-reel tape recorder someone had donated to the ministry. When I first sat in that closet talking to the tape recorder, I wondered if anyone would ever listen to the broadcasts. I didn't wonder long.

As soon as the tapes were broadcast, listeners in Taiwan began sending letters asking for prayer, requesting Bibles, telling how their lives had been changed.

I was especially moved by the letters from mainland China, smuggled out at great risk. The writers wrote how they hid in garrets and barns so they could tune in without being overheard by the authorities.

The response to the weekly programs was so great that we began broadcasting every day. We graduated from the walk-in closet to a much more sophisticated system in which taped programs were sent by air freight to Taiwan where they were broadcast over the powerful transmitters of the BCC.

One day as I opened a packet of letters from mainland China, I saw one addressed: "Personal—to the attention of Sung Neng Yee."

When I opened it I sat back in my chair, my thoughts travelling back into time when I left Red China in 1958. It was from my old friend, Mei-an to whom I had bid a heartfelt goodbye that night before leaving:

> I was so happy to hear your voice the first time on the radio. To learn that my Neng Yee never betrayed Jesus, but that she is still living for Him, and to hear that you found the blue-eyed, round-eyed people to love you.
>
> I've been tortured many times for my faith. There are scars all over my body where the Communists have burned me with hot irons. But I still love Jesus.

She went on to write that she knew it was difficult for me, leaving my family to travel so much.

> But don't ever be discouraged, my beloved. Never give up the work to which God has called you. Many underground churches have risen up because of your radio ministry. And your broadcasts have nourished the newborn Christians and helped them grow. The radio church is the only church a Chinese Christian can have, because it isn't safe for us to gather together to worship God . . . This may be my last letter, but don't cry for

me. I've given a Christian friend your address and told her where she can reach you if anything happens to me.

Tears filled my eyes as she wrote that she believed she had little time left.

Oh, Neng Yee, my last prayer will be that whatever happens to me, God will bless the church in America and keep the American Christians free, so they can have the Bible and worship God and keep on helping you tell the Chinese about Jesus.
Let all the Americans know how much we love them, and assure them that we'll meet in heaven some day. May Communism never touch them and take away their priceless freedom. . . .

She closed the letter by writing that someone was knocking on her door.

"God bless you forever," she concluded.

The envelope in which her last letter came was addressed in someone else's handwriting, blurred by tears. As I pressed her letter to my bosom, shuddering at what had happened to her and praying for her soul, I heard the Lord's voice: "Fear not, I am with You always. And I have overcome the world. You will be with Me in paradise."

I knew that my friend, Mei-an, had heard that Voice too.

Her letter gave me the strength to face a new challenge that lay ahead.

A TERROR NAMED
THELMA

Take Americans overseas with me?
I couldn't believe this was the Lord's direction.
"Why, Father?" I pleaded. "I don't want to be a tour guide. Besides, they're used to American food, which they won't find in Taiwan. The trip would be difficult."

But the Lord insisted. And in 1974 American pastors, deacons, doctors, lawyers, men and women in Christian fellowships, young, old, black and white, from all different denominations went to Taiwan with me.

To my surprise all of them loved the Chinese food and didn't complain about lack of luxuries. What they did do was help me with the ministry. Thousands of Chinese stormed the altar to receive the Lord. I could never have ministered to so many. But every American Christian with me was an extension of Jesus.

From then on I would never hold another crusade without taking along as many Americans as the planes could hold.

But with the expansion of my ministry, I found myself floundering. I saw the needs but didn't know how to meet them. The more I tried to do God's work, it seemed the less I knew about how to do it.

I needed help. And so I fasted and prayed seeking it. *Call Pat Robertson,* was the directive.

I knew who he was, but had never met him and was sure he didn't know me from Adam. But the Lord was insistent. So with fear and trembling I put the call through. When Pat answered the phone, I said: "I don't know why, but the Lord told me to call you."

"Is this Nora Lam?" he asked.

I almost dropped the phone. "How did you know?"

"While shaving this morning, Jesus told me you were going to call. I know who you are. I stayed up late last night to read your book."

What he said next almost made me hang up the phone.

"Nora, I need three and a quarter million dollars."

I couldn't even *think* about that much money, let alone help him get it. Not knowing what else to do, I said, "Let's pray." While we prayed I saw money falling from heaven like a snowstorm.

I told Pat I believed he would soon have all the money he needed. He thanked the Lord for what seemed like a half hour—on my phone bill. After we said goodbye, the Lord asked *me* to send one thousand dollars to Pat Robertson.

After vainly arguing that my little thousand dollars so badly needed for China would mean nothing in the face of three and a quarter million dollars, I sent Pat Robertson the check.

Not long afterward he called me to say that the Lord told him that if he wanted his great need to be met, to send ten thousand dollars to me! Then he asked me to fly to Virginia Beach to be on his "700 Club" TV program. On the program I told about how my thousand and Pat's ten thousand had traded places. I also confessed, "I wondered if Oral

Roberts preached about seed faith because he wanted others to send him their dollars. But now I have seen how it works. Oral knew God would help those who planted seeds for His work."

After that, listeners started sending a lot of seeds to the Christian Broadcasting Network to where Pat sent me *another* ten thousand dollars because, he said, God had already supplied the three and a quarter million dollars plus an additional $178,000!

With twenty thousand dollars, I was able to charter buses to bring twenty thousand school children from Buddhist families to our next crusade every afternoon. Each one asked for and received a Bible, and went home as missionaries to their parents, all because I had obeyed God and called Pat Robertson.

Then God asked me to do something else.

Go and buy TV time.

This time I didn't argue for by now I knew better. I flew to Taiwan and went straight to the office of China TV.

They ushered me into the office of the man in charge of selling time. When I told him what I wanted, he leaned back in his swivel chair, clasped his hands behind his head, and studied me with a quizzical look.

"Why didn't you call me long distance instead of making such a long trip?" he asked. Then leaning forward on his desk he said with a note of sarcasm in his voice, "And what made you think I'd even sell time to you? Your message has never been on China TV before." He sniffed. "There aren't that many Christians here, only three percent of the people."

"I know," I said. "I came in person because the Lord told me to do it. I guess He knew that if I telephoned long distance you'd say 'No' just like that, and that would be it."

He shook his head. "I can't give you a contract for time."

"Yes, you can," I insisted, half rising from my chair, "because God told me to buy it."

Anger flared in his eyes. "You come on too strong," he snapped. "It makes people not like you."

"Well, I'm sorry if they don't like me. But when God tells me to do something, I have to do it."

I was determined to sit there until he gave me what I had come for.

"A man who came to your crusade this year is really angry with you," he said. I could tell he wanted to change the subject to get me off the track.

"Who's angry at me?"

"A friend of mine," said the TV man. "He had a malignant brain tumor and came to your last crusade. He had to wait three whole days before getting on the platform for you to pray for him. When he finally reached you, he thought you'd spend at least a few minutes with him. But all you did was touch him on the head and say, 'In the name of Jesus be healed.'

"He was so disappointed that he went home angry at wasting so much time. Finally, he went to bed and during the night he began perspiring. The inside of his head got so hot he became frightened.

"The next morning he went to his doctor to find out what was happening. After examining him and taking some X-rays, the doctor told him his tumor had disappeared."

I started to say something but the Lord held my tongue.

The TV man leaned back in his chair, looked out the window, and shook his head slowly. "Now the man says he wants to get on television and tell about his healing."

The TV man's brow suddenly wrinkled. He leaned forward on his desk, picked up a letter opener and began thoughtfully studying it. I knew he had been trying to condemn me with that story but I could see the Holy Spirit was using it to convict him instead.

The man put down the letter opener, and looked up at me mystified. "I guess I should not fight you," he said.

"I guess not," I said softly.

"I guess I should sell you some time."

"I guess so."

We signed a contract for the first Full Gospel program on television in the history of Taiwan.

One of the first people to tell their story on our half-hour programs in 1976 was, of course, the man with the healed brain tumor. Afterwards we received two thousand letters from people throughout Taiwan who were touched by his story.

Again and again I marveled at the impact our radio and television broadcasts were having on people. Once, while I was answering reporters' questions in Taipei, a thin, frail woman tried to push her way up to me.

"I must see Nora," the woman cried. "I have brought her a gift."

I asked the people to let her through and counted nine stair-step children sticking close to her. Shyly, she thrust a bedraggled bouquet of wilted flowers into my hand.

"I wanted to thank you for what you have done for me and my family," she said. She looked full of joy, but so tired I found her a place to sit.

"I'm sorry the flowers have died," she said. "They were beautiful when we picked them before leaving home four days ago. And I'm sorry the children and I are so dirty from our journey."

I smiled at the children. They grinned bashfully, giggled, and tried to hide behind each other.

"It was just about a year ago . . ."

With that, the woman named Lee Sung Yu held me spellbound as she told her tragic story. Life had become unbearable for her, an impoverished widow. She and her family were starving and, giving up hope, she could see only one way out. Irrational because of malnutrition, she made a horrible decision. She would take the children one by one to a deep well near their hovel and throw them into it to die. Then she would leap in it herself and be through with the hunger and sorrow forever.

As the unsuspecting oldest boy followed her to the well, he had picked up their tiny transistor radio and stuck it inside his ragged shirt. Turning the dial, he accidentally tuned into one of my broadcasts. His mother heard my voice speaking directly to her:

"I'm the mother of three children. I was persecuted and tortured by the Communists, but God performed a miracle to let me escape from Red China. Mothers, wherever you are, let me tell you that Jesus, the Son of God, is the answer to all your problems. No matter how discouraged you might be right now, He can give you hope. Don't give up. Just wait on the Lord. He will help you. You and your kids belong to Him. He wants to take care of you."

As Lee Sung Yu listened, she fell to her knees beside the well and cried out to God, "I'm so helpless. Do for me what You did for the lady on the radio. You can have my life, but help me and my children."

She rose from her knees a new person with hope, knowing she could face the future. Instead of ending the lives of her children, she introduced them instead to the One who would save their lives forever.

With renewed hope and a reason for living, Lee Sung Yu was able to bring her family back from poverty. In her new enthusiasm, she found food where she thought it never existed before. She also became part of her community, sharing her new faith with neighbors.

After she told her story, I buried my face in her little

bouquet of wilted flowers and thanked her for renewing me also.

Individuals like her inspired me to keep our crusades going, even in spite of problems that threatened to ruin these effective outreaches.

Perhaps the most besieged crusade was in 1977, for which God had given me a vision: *Reach the children, use the media, reach the leaders.*

Obedient, S. K. and I went to Kaohsiung in late March to arrange for the summer meeting. We invited the mayor and other important leaders to sit on the platform. We rented seven hundred buses to bring children in from all over, including the remote mountain areas. And we arranged for the Christian Broadcasting Network to videotape the entire Crusade for later presentation on our television program.

On Sunday afternoon, July 24, opening day of the crusade, a steady rain began to fall. Weather reports said Typhoon Thelma threatened. But that didn't deter the people. The first meeting wouldn't begin until 7:30 P.M. but crowds began to arrive at four o'clock in the afternoon in spite of the rain which was getting heavier.

The 175 Americans with me were impressed. One declared, "In America, at the first sprinkle, everyone would have decided to stay at home."

The rain became a torrent, but the crowds continued to come. Soon the stadium was packed with over thirty thousand people pressed together in the wet bleachers under umbrellas. Still they came until many stood under the bleachers and outside the stadium where they could hear the message on the loudspeakers. When I gave the altar call about 9:30 that night, practically everyone raised their hands to say they wanted to pray the sinner's prayer and invite Jesus into their hearts.

This must have infuriated Satan, for later that very night Kaohsiung was hit with all the fury of one of the worst typhoons in its history. Winds of 125 miles per hour shook our hotel, and soon everyone was ordered to leave their rooms and go to the lobby, then to the basement.

After a time the storm subsided. Some of us on the crusade team went to inspect the stadium. I stood in shock; the arena was a complete wreck. The colorful bandstand where the mayor and other leaders had been seated was splintered wood. In utter despair, we headed to the indoor arena where the Children's Crusade was to be held the next afternoon. Even there, part of the roof was gone and there was water and debris everywhere.

"Should we just call off the meeting?" one of the team asked. We stared at the muddy ground wondering what to do. No one could blame us for giving up. The hotels would be without electricity or running water for days. There was no way to print a newspaper, no telephone service.

"God must be planning to do something big," another team member ventured, "otherwise, why would the enemy try so hard to stop us?"

I looked up at the angry dark clouds scudding across the gray sky. "Oh God, don't let a storm make us give up. You are bigger than any storm."

His answer came in the form of a growling roar and we looked at each other startled. The roar came from the stadium parking lot and when we got out there, three busloads of children had arrived from the mountains.

A teacher dismounted from the first bus, shaken and pale. "The wind wanted to blow us off the highway," he said. "Sometimes the rain came down so hard we could not even see. Many times the driver and I wanted to turn back as some buses had done earlier, but the children wouldn't let us do it."

From within the bus we could hear little voices clamoring: "We want to hear about Jesus! We want to hear about Jesus!"

The team members and I looked at each other, eyes

blurry with tears. We climbed onto the buses and gave Bibles to all the children. Some scriptures were soggy but the children were delighted.

"If you can spend the night in Kaohsiung and come back tomorrow, with God's help, there will be a meeting," we promised.

When the buses left, we called the other team members together and told them about the faith of the little children. Inspired, they all rolled up their sleeves and went to work, clearing away debris, sweeping water out of the building, and rigging up temporary lighting and sound systems.

The next afternoon more buses arrived and thousands of children heard about Jesus.

During the rest of the crusade our light and sound systems were makeshift, rain poured through holes in the roof, and despite the widespread destruction from the typhoon and disruption of travel, thousands streamed to the crusade to hear the Word of God. There was salvation and healings and tens of thousands of Bibles put into eagerly outstretched hands.

On the long flight back to the U.S., I thought about the vision God had given me months before.

Reach the children. He had done that more than we could have asked.

Use the media. TV cameras had captured the most dramatic Crusade of all.

Reach the leaders. On the last night, the mayor of Kaohsiung, who had been a Buddhist all his life, held a copy of *The Living Bible* in his hand and proclaimed, "This is the Word of God. We must get it to our people!"

And not long after we arrived home, God showed his power in another unusual way. I heard about it in an excited phone call from Johnson Han of the Bethany Children's Home where we helped build the swimming pool for which some criticized us.

Johnson Han said that on September 24 another typhoon struck Taiwan flooding the children's home area. The youngsters awakened screaming in terror as the flood waters swirled around their bunks. They climbed to their top bunks but still the water rose. There was only one escape. The larger younsters put the smaller ones on their backs, dived into the floodwaters and swam out of the rooms across the campus to safety in another building on higher ground. Not a single child was lost because all were good swimmers, thanks to the swimming pool.

Johnson Han went on to say that all the children said: "Tell Mama Sung to send us new Bibles, because we know it was Jesus Who built the swimming pool and taught us to swim so He could save our lives."

Again and again we continued to be surprised by the way God works. And I was never more amazed by what He did in 1978.

In January I had the opportunity for a most unusual intervIew on my television program. It was with Colonel Fan Yuen-yen, a Red Chinese squadron commander who had escaped to Taiwan in his Mig-19 fighter plane in July in 1977 to join the Nationalist Air Force of Free China.

His face clouded as he related the terrible conditions in Red China. Starvation was rampant, he said, and the people lived in constant fear.

It hurt to hear these things since my brother, Neng Yao, his wife, and child were still living under Communist oppression. Hundreds of people all over the United States had joined me in praying for their release. And one day I knew those prayers were being answered for He spoke to me:

Prepare to receive your brother Neng Yao and his family because I'm moving to set them free.

I was so excited; we bought a house behind us so they would have a place to stay. Our own house was full since S.K. and I had adopted two little Asian orphan girls by that time.

But nothing seemed to happen. Then my daughter-in-law, Paul's wife, Susie, phoned me quite excited. "Mom, I just saw on television that Senator Ted Kennedy is going to Mainland China. Ask him to help get your brother out."

But I demurred. Who was I to call a United States senator who didn't know me?

Then the Lord let me know in His inimitable way that I had to do my part.

Unless you step out in faith, the Spirit cannot act.

It made sense. I realized God wants to save the whole world, but He depends on missionaries to go tell the people the Good News. He cannot move until *we* move.

I called the senator's office. His assistant said they would do what they could, but I was not to be too hopeful. In the San Francisco Bay area alone, more than twelve thousand families had applied to get relatives out of Red China.

After several weeks I learned that the senator had contacted Communist China's minister of foreign affairs about our request. Then I learned that my brother and his family had been allowed to travel to Canton. But they didn't have exit permits. Now I knew God was working.

But it would be in His own time. Four months passed with no word from Neng Yao. On May 13, the day before Mother's Day, a letter came from him informing us the police had suddenly told him that he and his family should be ready to leave.

But then friends discouraged me. "Even if he does get out," one said, "it will be years before he can be approved as an immigrant to the United States."

On June 1 I went to the immigration office to apply for my brother to come to the United States. The next day his visa was in my hands.

But still we had not heard from Neng Yao. I worried about the Communist government; it was capricious. What they said one morning was often reversed by the afternoon.

However, I had to concentrate on our 1978 Crusade beginning in August. It would be the largest one yet. Hundreds of pastors, laymen and government officials would give leadership with over three thousand volunteer workers. One hundred buses were mobilized to bring in five thousand aborigines from the high mountains. Hundreds of churches in the Taipei area alone participated with seven hundred buses offering free transportation to anyone wishing to attend. Two hundred trained Chinese counselors and almost three hundred American workers were ready to pray with people. And two hundred thousand Chinese *Living Bibles* along with thousands of other books had been printed.

On opening day hundreds of buses unloaded swarms of enthusiastic people at the massive arena. As darkness settled, huge banks of lights flooded the farthest corners of the great green grassy soccer field. Television crews set up cameras to videotape the services for future television release. A powerful sound system was set up to convey every utterance in Mandarin and Taiwanese.

At the beginning of the crusade, thousands rose to sing hymns familiar to the sprinkling of believers in the vast congregation. A colorful aboriginal choir sang, then the beautifully robed Mandarin singers. Dr. Ralph Wilkerson of Melodyland Christian Center in Anaheim, California, presided and his wife played the organ. Singing star B.J. Thomas performed and gave his testimony of deliverance from drug addiction. Patti Roberts sang, and I preached the Word of God.

Lives were changed and renewed. Hundreds were healed and restored to health. This meeting was an experience I shall never forget, and one which prepared me for a miracle yet to come.

As I rested in my hotel room exhausted after the crusade, the phone rang. It was our travel agent saying due to an unexpected rerouting of our flight we'd have to change planes in Hong Kong.

Hong Kong! That's where my brother would enter the free world if he ever got out. Something moved me to call my aunt who lived there and to ask if anything could be done to speed Neng Yao's arrival.

"Neng Yee," she exclaimed. "I was trying to call you. Your brother and his family got out of Red China last night, and today they are in Hong Kong waiting to see you!"

What a reunion we had in the Hong Kong airline terminal. My brother who had been just a boy when I left China twenty years ago, was now a handsome man. With him stood his beautiful wife and their little black-haired, bright-eyed son, Mike.

When all of us reached home in California I could hardly wait to take Neng Yao into our mother's bedroom where she had been bedfast for some time.

"Mama, here is your son," I said, my voice breaking with emotion, as my tiny aged mother sat up in bed. She reached out to touch Neng Yao, straining to see him with eyes that had grown dim.

"Is this really my son? My baby?"

"Yes, Mama, this is your son. Your baby."

Her lined face was luminous with joy as she fondled his features. I thanked God that He had allowed her to live long enough to know her fervent prayers were answered, that her son was now in a land where he could worship Jesus freely and openly.

Then Neng Yao revealed something completely unexpected. Some time ago back in China, the Communists had contacted him saying they needed the land on which our father had been buried after his murder in 1957. They exhumed his body and called him to identify it. Later, they cremated the remains and gave his ashes to Neng Yao. The ashes were now in the United States awaiting our disposition.

As Neng Yao related this, it suddenly dawned on me that God's promise to me many years ago was now completely fulfilled.

Our whole family had gotten out of Red China!

But I did not know I would soon be going back.

INTO THE THROAT OF THE DRAGON

Probably the most shocking pronouncement from the Lord came Sunday evening, August 19, 1979, as I sat quietly in a church in Spokane, Washington.

On the road again raising funds for Bibles for the Far East, I was about to step onto the pulpit when His Word came.

It is time for you to return to Mainland China.

I gripped the arms of my chair not believing the Lord would ask me to return to the land from which I had barely escaped with my life. When the choir finished singing, I rose unsteadily to my feet and made my way to the pulpit. Grasping its sides for support, I reported in a shaking voice: "My heavenly Father has just told me to return to my homeland."

There were gasps from the congregation and then, without thinking further about what I could hardly comprehend, I preached. Later that evening I called home and told S.K. and the children. They were as shocked as I but said they would start arranging for a new passport and other details.

On the plane home to San Jose I wondered how the trip would ever be possible. It had been twenty-one years since

I left Red China. What contacts could I make? How would I ever find anyone? However, as we handled the possible, God accomplished the impossible.

In October I left the San Francisco airport with my friend, Mrs. Ralph Wilkerson, on a plane bound for Tokyo. There we would join a group of Americans for a ten-day visit to Mainland China.

Through a minor miracle I found I did have one contact there. By telephone I had been able to reach an old friend in Shanghai. Nancy promised to meet me in Beijing (originally Peking) and help me contact the underground church.

During the long overseas flight I had time to review developments in China during the years I was away. So much sorrow, so much bloodshed. Chairman Mao in 1966 had mobilized millions of young people called Red Guards. Encouraged to destroy any vestiges of the old ways, they denounced all "class enemies," which included educated and professional people, and went on a rampage in destroying the "old culture." They ricocheted completely out of control, and Mao finally had to call in the military to restore order, but tremendous damage had been done including a lost generation of young people. Then in 1971 China became a member of the United Nations with Taiwan losing out. A year later the United States established friendly relations with the mainland. In 1976 Chairman Mao died, and his ill-famed "Gang of Four," his four closest advisors, including his widow who had planned to seize power, were arrested. Since then, China has seemed anxious to modernize, to seek ways to build a strong nation.

That is why in 1979 it was open to us American tourists. Even so, I viewed our visit with dread. It was still a Godless country. And this was confirmed by the briefing given our group in Tokyo.

We were instructed to "behave as Christians," giving offense to no one, but not to indicate we had any official

Christian connection so as not to jeopardize the entry of other groups in the future.

We could bring a few Bibles in one small suitcase but could not offer them or other Christian literature to our guides, or people on the street.

Late Sunday afternoon, October 28, 1979, we flew from Tokyo to Beijing, the capital city where I had been born. As our plane touched down and taxied up to the terminal, I saw a Communist soldier in his red and green uniform, and my heart caught.

Once again I could hear the screaming questions, feel the backbreaking loads of coal under the burning sun, suffer the thirst, the hunger, see the blood-drenched sheets of my father's deathbed, hear the roar of the rifles as I stood before the firing squad.

"Have you any friends or relatives in China?" I was startled out of my thoughts by the man at the customs and immigration desk. It was midnight, and I was the last of our tour group to go through the line.

"Have you any friends or relatives in China?"

"I don't have any immediate family here," I shrugged.

"What will you be doing in China?"

"Visiting as a tourist," I answered. After a few more questions I stepped into mainland China, the land I had left twenty-one years ago as a forlorn refugee, bloated in my twelfth month of pregnancy, unaware of what lay ahead.

With two American friends, I hailed a taxi to find my old friend Nancy. When I had called her from California, she had told me where she would be staying in Beijing.

It took two hours of driving through back alleys and twisting narrow streets to finally find the address late that night. When we knocked on the door, Nancy opened it wearing a robe over her pajamas; she screamed with joy on seeing me.

We talked far into the night. And the next few days were full of unforgettable experiences.

The most poignant was driving up in front of the Wee Yo Hospital in Beijing where I had been born. As I stood looking up at its grimy, tile-roofed exterior I thought of my birth mother, who had to give me up because her highborn family would not allow her to marry her handsome opera-star lover. Later, I was happy to learn that she had eventually married and had other babies she could keep and love.

In Shanghai, now an overwhelming cosmopolitan metropolis, emotions swirled within me as I visited the old buildings that once were the Mary Farnham School where I first met Jesus. And once again I walked up the cobblestoned street leading to my step-grandmother's house which now housed a small factory.

One afternoon in Shanghai, toward the end of our visit, I was walking with some others to an evening meal at Nancy's second-floor apartment. We passed a ragged, toothless ancient woman, her gray hair in long hanging braids, struggling to push an ancient wooden wheelbarrow loaded with green vegetables over the cobble stones. Her humped shoulders were eloquent of sorrows, and her eyes stared dully with the hopelessness of a person without God.

I could not get her out of my mind that evening as my friends and I visited in Nancy's apartment. She had a piano and after dinner, Mrs. Wilkerson sat down to play it so we could all sing together. We sang songs celebrating Jesus such as "O Come All Ye Faithful" and "Silent Night." At first we sang softly so no outsider could report us. Then, something happened. The words brought courage to our hearts and strength to our voices. Soon we were singing loudly, enthusiastically, fearless of anyone who might be listening.

As we sang I thought of that poor old woman we had passed earlier in the evening. And I knew that with the Word of God in her heart, she would know the perfect love that casts out all fear, and with the knowledge that Jesus was with her, she would never be hopeless again.

I knew then that I would return to mainland China again and again on behalf of the millions of hopeless men and women like her.

And, as if in confirmation of how His Word would spread, one of my Chinese friends spoke up after we had finished singing.

"Nora Lam Sung, before you came and brought us the Word of God, I wanted with all my heart to get out of Red China, to leave this land where I've suffered so much and never to return again."

She opened her new Bible which we had given her and pressed it close to her heart. "But now, I want to stay forever and help my people know the living God."

And this is how it will be, like the old story, one beggar telling another beggar where to find bread.

As our jet liner hurtled through the night back to the United States, I knew I would return as often as the Lord would allow to bring Christ's freedom to my Chinese countrymen.

After my arrival home, two things happened which confirmed that feeling.

One was rereading a letter that Jim Gerrard had written to S.K. and me two years after he had first prophesied that God would use me in the Far East. In part, it read:

> God has told me He is opening a huge door
> involving the salvation of the Chinese. And He says,
> "When I open that Door, no man can shut it." There is
> coming a Holy Ghost bonfire sweep of souls into the
> Kingdom. It will spread like a prairie fire. People who do
> not see it will just not believe it. But you two shall see it,
> and believe it . . . for you fit into God's great plans . . .
> All the so-called power of the Communist rulers

on the mainland of China is as nothing compared to what God could do . . . God tolerates a thing just so long. And then He begins to prepare a man . . . or a woman . . . or a few men . . . to serve Him.

God does not need to wait for an "open door." He *creates* history. He opens doors.

God has a people in China. He always keeps a remnant. And He has heard the cries of His people. He has seen their afflictions.

. . . And He will move in ways of great wonders to save these people.

God showed me how easy it was to take a nation like Indonesia, and to deliver her from Communistic oppression. It was done by signs, miracles, and wonders . . . He told me plainly that He was going to do an Indonesian-type work in all of China . . .

Nora and S.K., I know that God has called you two! You are to be part of the great deliverance for China. God has already given you "tokens of His power." You know that if He sends you, He will be with you. . . .

(signed) Jim Gerrard

And not long after I had reread Jim's letter, another message came that filled me with an indescribable awe.

It came through my good friend Sue Westbrook of Fremont, California, the woman who so dramatically brought God's Word for me to return to Taiwan back in 1972. That was in the Assembly of God church in San Jose, California, where, kneeling next to me, she found herself giving His message in my native Mandarin, even though she knew no Chinese.

The message she brought to me after my return from Mainland China was even more dramatic. It came through her friend Mrs. Dearborn who taught in a Christian school and was taking a night class at Stanford University.

She happened to be seated next to a man from Mainland China. On learning he was a Christian, she asked him for his testimony. He seemed quite open about his experience and gave it straightforwardly, without embellishment:

"I was a sharpshooter in Communist China, assigned to a firing squad," he said. "One day a woman was brought before us who admitted to being a Christian. She wouldn't deny her God, but prayed aloud to Him during the last three minutes she had to live.

"We tried three times to shoot her, but each time we heard the count to fire, a brilliant light came down from the sky, blinding us. Our guns became almost too hot to hold and, as we squeezed the triggers, the guns were jerked upward by some unseen force. This happened three times.

"I knew that if I was unable to kill this woman, I would be killed myself, so I dropped my gun and ran. Miraculously, no one pursued me, and I escaped and found my way to a Catholic convent. The Sisters took me in. I told them I knew there was a God, and that I had been taught wrongly by the Communists, for I had seen Him at work when one of His followers called on His name.

"I wanted to know the kind of God that woman knew, that real God with real power. There in the convent I met Jesus."

When Sue Westbrook finished telling me what that rifleman had said, I sank to my knees in grateful comprehension. For it was a final confirmation from God that all my suffering back in China was part of His great plan.

Yes, if only this one soldier was helped by my witness, it was all worth it. More than ever, I dedicated myself to doing whatever I could to bring others to Jesus, the One who saved not only my life, but my soul. In committing myself unreservedly to sharing Him with a troubled and lost world, I travel millions of miles each year across America and China to reach people with the declaration of the everlasting gospel.

I hear the cry of China day and night. And I hear that

same cry for Jesus in America as well. In my journey of love and witnessing, I find opportunities daily to answer that cry; to tell people how to be an overcomer and live a victorious life; to give a cup of cold water in His name to the hurting, the needy, the lost. And also to let the privileged adrift in a sea of affluence know that yes, in Jesus they, too, can find the stimulating life they so fervently seek.

My wonderful adventure that began as a young girl in China has no end in sight. In fact, propelled by the everlasting love of God, it is on the threshold of its greatest beginning!

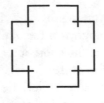

EPILOGUE

Late in May of 1989 my family and I were glued to the television watching one million Chinese students and workers demonstrating for freedom, reforms, and democracy in Tiananmen Square. Tiananmen meaning "Heavenly Harmony" seemed just that to my children—Paul, Ruth, Joseph, and their spouses.

As we watched the joyful students unfurl their colorful banners and parade their Goddess of Democracy statue around the square, my children were awed at the unbelievable possibility of what seemed to be happening.

"Are we watching a transition from oppression to democracy?" asked Joseph. Ruth's eyes were bright with hope, and Paul thought that finally the people of China would have a say in how they were governed.

There was one note of gloom struck in the room. It was by me.

"Wait and see," I said sadly. "The demonstration for freedom will reach a point to where, suddenly, party leader

Deng Xiaoping and his old comrades will crack down. There will be bloodshed soon in Tiananmen Square."

It was not a pleasant prophecy. But I had lived too long under Communist oppression not to know that the outcome would be any other way.

And, of course, there was tragedy in Tiananmen Square. It ran red with blood as thousands were shot, bayonetted, and crushed by tanks. For one bright moment the students' hopes and dreams were exemplified by that lone white-shirted man defiantly standing in front of a massive tank.

Some pundits say Tiananmen Square could not have ended in any other way. It had taken the Communists almost half a century to weld the long-fragmented country together. They were afraid if the demonstration got out of hand their effort could fly apart like a clay pot on a wildly spinning potter's wheel.

Others disagree. They say that if the students and workers were listened to, China would be a much stronger, more united nation today.

I do not have any prediction one way or another.

For as my Leader says: "My kingdom is not of this world."

Since Jesus' birth two thousand years ago, hundreds of mighty empires have risen and fallen. Governments have been founded for "a thousand years" only to vanish in decades.

So I continue serving Him by helping bring freedom to the oppressed, victory to the vanquished, hope to the hopeless.

In China, despite Tiananmen Square, I see that hope growing.

"Without doubt there's a spiritual crisis in China," said a university student in Beijing in a *New York Times* article of May 18, 1990. He said some of his friends were turning to religion as a new source of moral values.

"I don't have any friends who believe in Marxism

now," he added. "Even my parents don't believe in Marx or Deng Xiaoping anymore. There's a vacuum."

I see this hunger for something spiritual in the sweeper in the Shanghai railroad station, in the oarsman on a sampan in the Whangpoo River, in the students and leaders of the universities. The U.S. Center for World Missions recently reported: "More than 20,000 Chinese people are coming to Jesus every day." Once a person has a spiritual faith in which he can trust, he is truly free, no matter what kind of government he is subject to.

And so I continue working for Him.

CRUSADES TO CHINA

Twice a year, some two hundred and fifty or more lay Christians from North America travel with me on crusades to China and nearby Asian countries to minister. To date, some five thousand people have participated in these two-week evangelistic adventures in critically important cities.

In the past, thousands of Chinese attended mass evening rallies to hear our teams speak for Christ. We also visited hospitals, prisons, and factories during the day in presenting the gospel. Local Asian church leaders have opened their pulpits to us, and we have fellowshipped with congregations of both the house church movement and the Three Self Patriotic Movement State Church.

Many crusade-team members report the trip has changed their lives. They have discovered a deeper inner faith, an untapped spiritual power, and hidden charismatic gifts they never realized they had.

On a typical tour in 1988, over one hundred Americans, representing twenty-five different denominations and twenty-two states, visited with Chinese Christians in Canton, Nanjing, and Beijing. Interestingly, this group walked through customs in Canton carrying four thousand Chinese Bibles without a single Bible bag opened by the police.

We met openly with top Christian leaders including Bishop H. K. Ting of the state-approved Three-Self Patriotic Movement Protestant Church, leading pastors of the unregistered house-church movement and many Catholic bishops and clergy.

Team members distributed Christian literature and witnessed one-on-one to people throughout the trip and led a number of them to Christ. On several occasions, including an unforgettable experience atop the Great Wall, we held open-air worship without interference by the watching Communist officials.

We also were permitted to use four public halls in which we held cultural-exchange concerts featuring Dino Kartsonakis, the famed gospel pianist. These included the Great Hall of the People, and one in Beijing University. Some 5000 Chinese, including music students, university faculty and government officials, attended these standing-room only concerts.

Our crusade group also visited the Nanjing Theological Seminary where Bishop Ting, the official head of the Chinese church, met with us for Holy Communion. He revealed that two new churches were opening every three days under the then-lessened government restrictions.

In Shanghai, the city most familiar to me, we sang with senior citizens and visited Chinese families in their homes. Many young people found Christ as their Savior in meetings in our hotel rooms. Filled with the Holy Spirit, they were baptized in our bathtubs, something that happens often on our crusades. There must be hundreds of such "sanctified" hotel bathtubs in China by now.

Yet as wonderful as this all sounds, we must remember that out of the one billion Chinese people, the most optimistic estimate of the number of Chinese Protestant Christians is only fifty million. And that means Christians amount at best to only one half of one percent of the total mainland population!

Our ministry plans to conduct these crusades twice a year as long as the Lord allows them.

What happened after the massacre of Tiananmen Square?

Satan did everything he could to stop us. Because some critics spread lies about our past visits, my visa for our 1989 trip was denied three heart-breaking times, first in August, then October, and again early in December. Finally, through the efforts of former White House staffer Carolyn Sundseth and Doug Wead, former Special Assistant to President George Bush, the White House interceded on our behalf. On Christmas Day 1989, the Beijing government granted my visa; what a Christmas present!

Over seventy North American lay leaders joined us on this mission to Beijing, Nanjing, Shanghai, and Hong Kong. Our group was able to speak and sing in the Three Self Patriotic Movement churches where we noticed the youngest of the five pastors was age sixty-five. There is obviously a crisis of leadership in Chinese churches which desperately need young ministers today.

Then we went to tragic Tiananmen Square. Six months had gone by since the massacre, but marks of tank treads could still be seen on the pavement. And martial law was still in effect. We gathered to pray asking God to show mercy on the Chinese leaders and not bring judgment. We poured healing oil on the once-blood-drenched pavement as we prayed. Six days later the government lifted martial law in Beijing! I believe God had ordained our little mission.

Another breakthrough came Sunday, December 31, 1989, when the Chinese government invited us to meet with their Religious Affairs Bureau in Beijing, the powerful Communist office in charge of China's churches. This had never happened before. The purpose for the meeting was to "clear up misunderstandings" about why my visa was delayed.

But, again God worked it all out in a wonderful way. For we were able to exchange views in a positive light. And we learned that the government approved the Nora Lam cultural exchange program we have been operating through the years.

Yes, God had His Hand on our post-Tiananmen Square trip.

WHAT ABOUT BIBLES FOR CHINA?

The need is critical. Some have pointed out that the Amity Foundation which publishes Bibles in China fills the need. Though it has accomplished a real breakthrough, the need is far from being filled.

After forty years of Bible burning, the one book Communists fear more than any other is still available only to a select few. Amity Bibles are given only to the five million members of the Three-Self Patriotic Movement (TSPM) churches. This means that an estimated forty-five million "house church" Christians and Chinese Catholics are still without Bibles.

Even then, it will take over seven years just to print Bibles for TSPM church members. At this rate it will take another thirty-five years for those presently Christian to get their own Bibles. Only twelve thousand Bibles were available on the open market last year, and they disappeared as fast as they went onto bookstore shelves.

Because the average Chinese citizen is without access to the most influential book ever written in world history, our Bibles-for-China program is one of our most active ministries. Some of our methods of distribution involve the use of couriers from Hong Kong and family members in Taiwan with many of the Bibles being smuggled through the Canton border.

We concentrate on the *Living Bible* as the one most easily understood by unsaved people. And I'm proud of this comment from Ken Taylor, originator of the *Living Bible* and Director of Living Bibles International.

"Nora Lam has placed hundreds of thousands of Chinese *Living Bibles* into the hands of her own people. God is using her ministry to provide enlightenment to many through His Word."

WOULD YOU LIKE TO BE A SPECIAL KIND OF MISSIONARY?

You may already know that one of the Chinese government's highest priorities is for their students to learn English. In fact, in most major cities there are areas where students seek out Americans just to practice their English. The government realizes that foreign English teachers are a critical step in its drive to modernize China and catch up economically with the rest of the world.

Thus Chinese colleges and universities have asked our ministry to recruit and send American English teachers to the mainland. About ten thousand more such English teachers are needed.

This offers a wonderful opportunity for Christian witnessing. Most teachers we have sent over are seeing real spiritual fruit in helping to train the next generation of Chinese leadership.

To recruit and train these missionaries, our ministry screens, trains, and equips each English teacher. Most Americans with a college degree can learn how to tutor Chinese students, scholars, technicians, and scientists in about six weeks.

Once a teacher arrives in China, the government will pay him or her a salary adequate to live on in the local economy as well as provide other benefits including free housing and medical care.

A miracle in this is that Chinese Communist officials are pleased with the quality of Christian teachers who they find honest, ethical, and possessing the high moral standards that are most appreciated by their academic and government leadership.

Yes, China is reaching out, wanting us to come and teach their students English. And we can also bring many of them to Jesus if we are willing to be led by the Holy Spirit.

One such example is Nancy Smith, a young woman from Bremerton, Washington. For years she dreamed of going to China and reaching out with the love of Jesus to the people. But visa restrictions and red tape made a "normal" missionary career there unthinkable.

But through one of our ministry programs, she was accepted to teach college in Canton. She was so busy and involved in the lives of her students that she spent weekends and holidays in their rural homes.

"It's worth it for Americans to come here," she says. "The Chinese appreciate and want us here!"

What is Chinese life like for her? She says at the beginning it was like her first camping experience. She still does all her own laundry by hand, rides her bike everywhere just like the Chinese students do. She has her own bedroom, bathroom and kitchenette on campus, all provided free by the government. Her color TV, bicycle, medical care, and living allowance are also provided by the government.

Everything, she says, is modest and at the same level as her students—but this makes it easier for her to build friendships and serve.

"I couldn't ask for a better opportunity to serve people," says Nancy. "And that's the best thing.

"People here are ready to hear things about God. They want to know if there's more to life. That's why I don't feel like I can ever go home. There are so many people here who want what I have."

She says that holidays like Christmas prompt students to ask her what the real meaning of the holiday is and they even learn carols like *Silent Night* and *Joy to the World*.

"This year we were allowed to share the Christmas message for the first time at a school assembly," she says, "and the school officials who knew what we were going to say in advance gave us their permission and blessing."

TELEVISION BREAKTHROUGH

Our broadcast communications program continues in Taiwan and reaches mainland China. But probably our most exciting ministry is beamed *inside* mainland China under the auspices of its government's Central China Television project.

It all began in 1988 when I dreamed of reaching the Chinese people in a most effective way.

How could I do it? I prayed.

Television, He seemed to say.

"But Lord," I quavered. "The only television in China is government sponsored. They wouldn't allow *me* to be on their network.

There are other ways of reaching my children.

But how? I wondered.

Think Nora, think.

Then it came to me. What did Chinese people and their government want? To keep up on the latest developments in the world.

Why not a cultural exchange program covering topics of the day? I wondered. On it I could interview interesting personalities in sort of a talk program, like the TODAY Show in the United States.

Early negotiations with CCTV (Central China Television) seemed promising, and I was invited to their headquarters to meet with broadcast officials. As I walked up to the huge gray mass of buildings housing China's only television network, I thought about the angry government official who hurled my exit permit at me thirty years ago ordering me to "Never come back to China!"

Now, thanks to the workings of God, here I was in the middle of the Communist nation arranging to be on the country's giant television network. I would be used to help bridge the communications gap between America and China.

As I walked up to the CCTV's formal-looking doors, my heart pounded with excitement. What a thrill! What a glory for God! After our meeting, I arranged to have two top CCTV leaders flown to the United States to meet with Dr. Paul Crouch of the Trinity Broadcasting Network. The contracts for the China TV program were signed between the Chinese and TBN on November 17, 1987, in Santa Ana, California. And the first program aired in 1988 with my serving as the host person. One of the first shows was a lively interview with Paul Crouch and his wife, Jan, both well-known American Christian broadcasters. Subsequent programs featured other interesting personalities along with topics of the day, such as the progress of American space-shuttle flights.

Today, the program runs regularly reaching one of the largest audiences on earth with a potential viewership of 600 million.

Naturally, we cannot overtly preach on the program. But I take every opportunity to present God's truth in a subtle way. The response to this has been amazing. Many Chinese already know me through my evangelistic radio programs beamed from Taiwan. But then simply obeying Christ and acting as He would want me to evidently shines through. For huge bags of mail constantly come from mainland viewers with letters attesting to how God can speak between the lines. Here is one from a viewer in Shanghai:

Dear Nora Lam:
First of all, I want to thank God Who has linked us together, although we are thousands of miles apart physically. Three years ago I did not know God, and you brought us Bibles and literature from America. Through these materials, I was led to God and was baptized as a Christian. I want to hear your preaching of the Gospel. I watched you on TV introducing American communications. Last week my son watched you on TV. He called me immediately. You were introducing the American culture to us. I called my friend to watch the show. Although I have a black and white TV, I enjoyed watching your program. I hope I can hear your preaching personally.

A.M.S. (Shanghai, China)

A letter like this means more to me than any high Nielsen rating or television Emmy award.

REVIVAL IN CHINA

Yes, revival is burning like wildfire across the Chinese plains. And I believe God is preparing hearts now for the greatest spiritual move in China ever. Though there is currently great persecution in China, we know historically the Christian church has somehow always flourished under persecution.

Americans: We must plant our tears in Chinese soil. We must continue to pray for the Chinese people. More than anything I want to help bring better understanding between the people of the United States and China, to enhance the fascination both cultures already have for each other, to strengthen the bond between both peoples, which transcends any ideology, and which will continue regardless of political circumstances.

I think about the seeds of Christianity sown by such

great missionaries to China as Hudson Taylor. I remember China's own eminent writer and teacher, Watchman Nee, and I wonder, without their sacrifices, dedication, and obedience, plus the many who gave their lives so China might have the Word of God, where would I be today?

I doubt I would have had the faith to endure the torture and the trials I encountered.

Yes, America has cast its bread of hope and truth across the waters, and I pray that in some way I can minister hope and joy to Americans in return. To this end I minister constantly across the United States in our Miracle Breakthrough banquets. We are also vulnerable here in our country. For where it is not dangerous to be a Christian, people tend to become complacent. Then it is easy for the enemy to step in and before we realize it, our freedoms disappear. So as I speak at our banquets across the United States, my chief goal is to bring people to Jesus, and be resolute in their faith. I want hurting people to know that there is nothing too hard for our Lord to accomplish. There is no situation however threatening or grave that can conquer you when you put your trust in Christ.

He that dwelleth in the secret place of the most High shall abide under the shadow of the Almighty.
I will say of the Lord, He is my refuge and my fortress: my God; in Him will I trust (Ps. 91:1–2).

Yes, God sees every situation, every hurt, every disappointment and stands ready to forgive and to heal you.

Tiananmen Square will come and go, governments will rise and fall. Only Jesus Christ will remain as King. Thirty-two years ago I was a helpless refugee fleeing China. Today, through the grace of God and with your help, I return to China as His disciple, and preach throughout the United

States, to help everyone share in the riches of His kingdom. And now He has given us another way to share His message.

THE MIRACLE MOVIE, *CHINA CRY*

Yes, miracles are still happening. My true story was filmed on location in Hong Kong, Macao, and Hollywood, and premiered in Hollywood on November 1, 1990, at the famous Mann's Chinese Theater. The following day, it was released to more than two hundred theaters in twenty-three cities throughout the United States.

The miracle is that the film was made at all. Movie critics said that a picture like this could not be done. "A religious film won't be accepted in the mainstream market," argued one. "Too many miracles, unbelievable," said another. "Films about faith are not popular anymore," claimed a media expert. And on it went.

What happened? More than one million tickets were presold to eager patrons long before the film came out. *Variety*, the secular entertainment newspaper, reported, *"Cry* initially seems a strong bet for family entertainment . . . has several strong points to recommend it . . . boasts a stirring femme character portrait and sparkling performance by Julia Nickson-Soul," who played the lead.

The *Los Angeles Times* gave lavish coverage to *China Cry* and quoted PBS film critic Michael Medved, who called it "a very professional piece of work." As with all critics, the reviewers were candid at times, but one comment stands out: "It will ultimately help the cause of Christ and film evangelism."

It all began when CCTV (Central China Television) wanted a miniseries on me because of the interest generated by programs shown there. Paul Crouch, founder of Trinity Broadcasting Network, was going to do the series until he sensed God leading him to produce a major motion picture instead, for national and later worldwide release. TBN had never produced a motion picture before, and movies are frightfully expensive to make. Where would the money come from? Paul Crouch shared his vision with TBN viewers, and more than six million dollars in donations poured in.

"The people who sent in the money did it just to see this style of film made and have the joy of being part of it," said Crouch, who became its executive producer. He said it was also part of his desire to return inspiring family fare to cinemas.

Another miracle was getting James Collier (of the movie *The Hiding Place*) to write and direct it, and Tim Penland to oversee the film's distribution.

Our hope is that eventually *China Cry* will be shown in mainland China. What a powerhouse of a witness it will be!

Too much to ask, you think? Too much to expect, even of our Almighty God? No, nothing is too much for our God.

As you have read, He is a God of miracles. He has worked them in my life, and if you have faith, He will work miracles in your life too!

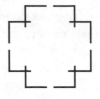

ABOUT THE AUTHORS

Dick Schneider, Senior Staff Editor of *Guideposts* Magazine, has written fourteen books including *I Dared to Call Him Father, Freedom's Holy Light, The Honorable Alcoholic,* and *Why Christmas Trees Aren't Perfect.* Married, with two sons, he lives in Rye, New York.

Nora Lam, whose story is told in these pages, continues to lead evangelistic crusades in the U.S. and China. If you would like to learn how to be an overcomer with Jesus, or want to know more about China, please write or call Nora Lam Ministries, P.O. Box 24466, San Jose, California 95154, (408) 629-5000.